TOTAL CREATIVITY
in Business & Industry

Road Map to Building
a More Innovative Organization

David Tanner

Tools, Processes,
Frameworks

Diversity in
Styles & Preferences

Engaging the Organization

Organizational
Systems & Structures

Champions & Supports

Ideas to Market

© 1997 by David Tanner

For information or to purchase multiple copies at volume
discounts address the publisher:

 Advanced Practical Thinking Training, Inc.®
10520 New York Avenue
Des Moines, IA 50322

Cover design by Sue Bjork and Connie Bever

ISBN 0-7807-6799-3 hardcover
ISBN 0-7891-2194-8 paperback

Dedication

To the "champions" everywhere striving for

creative excellence in everyday innovation

and

In memory of Jean P. Prideaux,

the exemplary champion, and

Richard S. Reese, the exemplary supporter

Acknowledgments

Working on this book brought back memories of the first time I heard Edward de Bono's Lateral Thinking seminar in Toronto, Spring 1986. I sat excitedly at the edge of my seat the whole time, inspired about the opportunities his teachings would open to me personally and to DuPont. Similarly, Ned Herrmann's ACT-I Workshop, which I attended at about the same time, had a profound impact on me personally and later on in DuPont. Over the years, other stimulative influences were provided by Stan Gryskiewicz, Scott Isaksen, Gifford Pinchot, Roger von Oech, and more recently Morris Stein. The teachings of these leaders in the creative-thinking field run throughout the book.

Equally important as the teachers are the practitioners and supporters. I refer here to the contributions of the many DuPont company champions and supports at all levels in the organization that made this book possible. Chapter VIII is devoted to this subject, describing the vital contributions of Jean Prideaux, Dick Reese, and others. Among the champions are the six DuPonters who in 1986 helped found the DuPont OZ Creative Thinking Network described in Chapter VII: Corey Ericson, Jim Green, Jim Magurno, Charlie Prather, Tim Weatherill, and Nat Wyeth.

Regarding the book itself, I am grateful to Edward de Bono, Ned Herrmann, and Morris Stein for writing such thought-provoking forewords that in themselves make the book worth reading. Other important contributors:

Richard Tait, who enthusiastically coauthored Chapter IX, "Taking Ideas to Market."

Michael Kirton and Ned Herrmann, who constructively edited the sections related to their work on diversity in thinking, Chapter V.

David Sixton and Claire Eeles, who championed the creativity and innovation efforts of the Fletcher Challenge company described in Chapter VII.

Bob Thaves, who kindly supplied the Frank and Ernest cartoons.

Kathy Myers, who unrelentingly encouraged the author to put in writing a book focused on the practical application of creativity techniques.

My wife, Lee Tanner, who constructively critiqued each section of this book.

During most of man's literate history, creative behavior has been thought to be artistic behavior and rather especially the writing of poetry, although the work of painter and sculptor were recognized early as being in the same class. The view that creativity is a matter of artistry, the process by which the artist produces his art, has only in relatively recent years been expanded to include the idea that scientists as well as many others in their endeavors can also be creative persons employing as does the artist the creative process.

Donald W. MacKinnon, University of California

Contents

Foreword by Edward de Bono

Foreword by Ned Herrmann

Foreword by Morris Stein

Foreword

Edward de Bono—London, December 1996

There are three aspects to creativity.

The first aspect is that organizations have to realize that they need creativity. Housekeeping and competence are not going to be enough in the future. Information and competence will become commodities. Creativity is essential in order to create new value. Creativity is not a peripheral luxury but the most important ingredient in business in the future. Most chief executives have not yet realized this. In any self-organizing information system, such as the human mind, there is a mathematical need for creativity.

The second aspect is to understand the nature of creativity. There is far too much rubbish written about creativity. A lot of it is fluffy, flaky, off-the-wall stuff. Just being liberated does not make a person creative. The brain is specifically designed to be uncreative. If it were otherwise, life would be impossible. We need to design deliberate creative tools (lateral thinking), which we can apply systematically and deliberately. We can build up skill in the use of such tools. Even the simple six-hat framework for parallel thinking produces huge gains in thinking productivity (up to five-fold increases). There is also a need to move on from a concern with "what is" (measuring tendencies and abilities) to "what can be" (training in methods and skills). A fat man can learn to ride a bicycle and outpace a thin man without a bicycle.

The third aspect is the introduction and application of these creative methods into an organization. The powerful contribution of David Tanner has been in this third area. Coming to realize for himself the key importance of creativity, David undertook the task of introducing it in a serious way into a major organization. That required energy, commitment, people skills, and political skills. Without this practical application, the tools and methods of creativity simply do not get used, and ideas are not taken up.

David Tanner clearly understands the field of creativity, but he goes beyond this in his ability to get others and organizations to take up and use the skills. I have watched the effective way he does this over the years.

Editor's note: There are over 4,000,000 references to the work of Edward de Bono on the Internet. His own Creative Team can be accessed at http://www.edwdebono.com.

Foreword

Ned Herrmann

Author, *The Creative Brain* and *The Whole Brain Business Book*

Past President of the American Creativity Association

For business applications, the bottom line of creativity is business results. This requires not only being creative, but applying creativity, championing it, and learning from those results how to do it better. There are many books on creative theory, but very few on creative applications for business. That is what makes this book so unique. It is written from the perspective of a corporate user, who, as the holder of 33 patents, is not only creative himself, but who has also held senior technical leadership positions in one of the world's great corporations. This is an ideal experience base from which to write this book. With freedom to choose from the wide universe of creative theories, techniques, and processes, Dave Tanner has chosen to write about only the ones that have worked best for him. In this book, there are over 20 specific creative processes and proven techniques, and over 60 application examples that take creativity out of the realm of creative theory and into the business domain of solving everyday problems.

In order for creativity to be successfully applied in business, it has to be accepted as part of the daily culture of the organization. This is not only rare, but it doesn't happen all by itself. It requires champions in key positions throughout the organization. Dave has made this clear by dedicating his book to his favorite creative champion, Jean Prideaux. What is not explicitly stated, but can be read between the lines, is why Dave Tanner himself is my nominee for the ultimate corporate level creative champion. What he did in his official position in DuPont is well described in this book. What is not described is how he impacted the entire culture of his company by inspiring many hundreds of employees, at all levels, to claim their creative potential and apply it at work. He did this by being a creative champion himself. By his example, he has given permission, not only to all of his former employees and associates, but also to the readers of this book, to claim their own creative space and exercise their own creative potential.

Foreword

Morris I. Stein, Ph.D.

Author, *Stimulating Creativity* (2 volumes) and *Making the Point*
Professor Emeritus, Psychology, New York University

In the mid-1990s, the management of research and development in American industry is involved in a paradigmatic shift from Planful Enabler to Determined Zealot. Enabler and Zealot seek improvements in our quality of life and their company's bottom line. But even as they share these goals, they differ in style, in process, and in the organizational climates they generate.

The Planful Enabler develops an organizational climate in which creativity is highly valued and appropriately rewarded. Opportunities are provided to engage in creative pursuits, and learning about the creative process is encouraged as a lifelong endeavor. The Planful Enabler manages but, more importantly, leads. He has a proven track record of creative accomplishments respected by superiors, peers, and subordinates. For many of them, he becomes a model to be emulated. Professional relationships are marked by mutual respect. The Planful Enabler knows the pain of "dry periods," plateaus, and even the depression that may occur during the creative process. Hence, he responds empathetically and constructively when he witnesses others experiencing similar difficulties. The Planful Enabler is nurturing without being paternalistic. The Planful enabler has high standards, which he achieves by facilitating each move to self-actualization and creativity.

The Determined Zealot is in a constant state of vigilance. He is always looking over his shoulder to see how fast the opposition is closing in on him—and it is. If the competition is not realistically breathing down his neck, it is imagined. Peers and subordinates are made acutely aware of how close they are to being overcome and surpassed. Threats, implicit and explicit, and humorless sarcasm are commonplace. "Have lunch or be lunch!" is the battle cry. "What have you done for me lately?" is the constant question. Efficiency is crucial. Productivity and creativity are often confused. Everyone's focus is on the bottom line. Commodities produced have a price, and so do people. People are frequently regarded as expendable and interchangeable. Creative works are produced with pressure— and with pressure, profits are also increased.

Planful Enablers and Determined Zealots have always existed. Enablers probably outnumbered Zealots in the not-too-distant past, especially when R & D managers were encouraged to be leaders. But times are changing. The values that shape the conduct of R & D organizations shift with the values of the broader society. The importance of the bottom line looms larger and larger. Economies are emphasized at all levels. There is a commodification of human relationships.

My guess is that the Determined Zealot is likely to become more prevalent. The Planful Enabler may become an endangered species. History tells us, however, that no leadership style ever disappears completely. It hibernates and remains dormant until conditons change, and then it comes to the fore again.

The book before you is a critical record of what one Planful Enabler undertook and what he and his associates were able to accomplish. It is also a plan and a guide for all those in industrial and educational organizations who want to bring the future into today.

During the first seven years of David's employment at DuPont, his research led to 33 U.S. patents. He then held a series of management jobs at several DuPont sites. In the 1980s, he became Technical Director, DuPont Industrial Fibers Technical Division, responsible for Research and Development in seven DuPont businesses: Kevlar®, Nomex®, Tyvek®, Sontara®, Teflon®, industrial nylon, and Dacron®.

Before long, it became apparent that DuPont's competitors were catching up. Rather than getting paranoid and putting pressure on his associates and subordinates from afar, Tanner, respecting their qualities and abilities, planned on restimulating their "creative juices."

I won't go into detail, because I don't want to give the plot away. I do want to point out, however, that a unique characteristic of this book is that when David Tanner talks about accomplishments, he names names and the effects they had on the bottom line. Therefore, readers who are already "believers" will find here reinforcement for their "faith"; skeptics, especially after reading Chapters VI and VII, should beware—they are likely to become converts.

Introduction

In his 1926 classic, *The Story of Philosophy*, Will Durant wrote:

> *Of theory and practice; one without the other is useless and perilous; knowledge that does not generate achievement is a pale and bloodless thing, unworthy of mankind. We strive to learn the form of things not for the sake of forms but by knowing these forms, the laws, we remake things in the image of our desire. So we study mathematics in order to reckon quantities and build bridges; we study psychology in order to find our way in the jungle of society.*[1]

Will Durant's philosophy about theory and practice holds true in the creativity field. Much has been written about the techniques of creative thinking. The value lies in applying these to solve problems and search for new opportunities.

Total Creativity in Business & Industry is about the practical application of creative-thinking techniques and a road map to building a more innovative organization. Six dimensions in creative thinking are described that help the reader understand how to:

1. Learn and apply creative-thinking tools, processes, and frameworks that provide the fuel for innovation leadership.
2. Capitalize on the value of diversity in thinking preferences and styles in building successful teams.
3. Engage the organization so that people will surface who have a clear idea of the values of the initiative and want to take part.
4. Set up structures and systems to sustain momentum in the initiative.
5. Recognize and reward emerging champions and supports.

6. Take best ideas to market, applying key components
   of the innovation process.

Creative thinking is a skill that can be learned and applied in
everyday innovation, even if people do not perceive themselves as
being creative. Like most skills, it takes time to learn the basics
and apply them to real situations. Attending a creativity seminar
or workshop or reading a book is a good start but seldom yields
instantaneous results.

An essential ingredient in implementing a creativity and
innovation effort in an organization is to create a supportive
environment reinforced with structures and systems. This
engages the organization, encourages ongoing learning, and
enables people to "dance with their ideas" in tackling difficult
issues. Over time, champions emerge, apply their learnings in
their jobs, and achieve rewarding results. These champions
become role models that nucleate other practitioners and
champions. Support by middle and upper management is vital to
success.

The author first became involved in the creativity field in the
mid-1980s as Technical Director responsible for research and
development in the DuPont Industrial Fibers Technical Division.
At that time, this division was operating in an environment of
much change and competitive pressure, particularly from
Japanese and European companies. Basic patents covering
technology for the growth businesses, i.e., Kevlar®, Tyvek®,
Sontara®, were expiring. Mature businesses, i.e., Nomex®,
Teflon®, industrial nylon, and Dacron® were leveling off.
Aggressive, "total quality" programs were underway pursuing the
principles of Juran, Deming, and Crosby. These were essential
but clearly not enough! It was time to place higher priority on
"total creativity" to generate entirely new concepts and ideas.

Creative-thinking techniques were introduced, learned, and
applied across the division over a period of four to five years.
There were many examples of bottom-line payoff. Corporate
management took note and sought to extend this knowledge
company-wide, which led to the DuPont Center for Creativity &
Innovation.

Introducing the skills of creative thinking into an organization is
usually resisted as just another time-consuming program.
Enabling a supportive environment is akin to culture change,

and it takes patience and time. This book describes the author's experience in facing these challenges, first as a Technical Director and later as Director of the DuPont Center for Creativity & Innovation. In reflection, the "total creativity" effort evolved into a six-dimensional approach, which is how this book is structured.

Early chapters orient the reader to the concept of creative thinking as a skill; consider the role of creativity in problem solving, innovation, and quality improvement; and explore the first two dimensions of building a creative organization: (1) creativity tools, processes, and frameworks found to be the most productive, with many examples of successful application; and (2) the importance of diversity in thinking preferences and creativity styles.

Later chapters describe the remaining dimensions: (3) the approach taken to engage the organization in a creative-thinking effort through enabling a supportive environment; (4) the structuring and operation of a corporate creativity and innovation center, including a Facilitator Network and the DuPont OZ Creative Thinking Network; (5) the importance of champions and supports; and (6) taking ideas to market, including five DuPont innovations ranging from Kevlar® to crawfish bait.

The book includes 18 productive creativity techniques and 58 examples of practical application. Thirty-one Frank and Ernest cartoons by Bob Thaves add a light touch to a serious subject. While most of the book is based on experiences within DuPont, several of the applications are based on the author's experiences serving as a consultant to other companies.

In the search for excellence in applied creativity, participants in the effort described in this book interacted with gurus in the field; audited workshops; tested tools, processes, and frameworks; benchmarked best practices; participated in creativity and innovation networks; and applied what they learned on the job. The author hopes that insights gained in this effort will be of practical value to readers of this book. The beauty of the creative-thinking field is that, unlike proprietary "hard" technology, creativity is a "soft" technology that can be shared.

Recognizing Creative Thinking as a Skill

If you think creativity is a mysterious gift, you can only sit and wait for ideas. But if creativity is a skill, you ought to learn it.

> Edward de Bono

To discuss creative thinking as a skill, let's first define *creative thinking*, starting with a story.

The story is about a chicken farmer and a town doctor. The farmer's chickens were dying, so he went to the town doctor to ask for help. The doctor said he could indeed help. He suggested that the next time the farmer feeds the chickens he grind up some vitamin C and sprinkle it on the chicken feed. The farmer returned a week later reporting that he had followed the doctor's directions, but that his chickens were still dying. Next, the doctor suggested increasing the humidity in the chicken coop. But the chickens continued to die. Next, the doctor suggested playing classical music in the chicken coop. The farmer did this, but when he returned to the doctor, he reported that all the chickens had died. The doctor replied, "I am sorry to hear that—I still had some original ideas to try."

Was the town doctor creative? When this question is asked of a group of people, there is a mixed response. Usually, about half reply "yes" and the other half "no." But there is no right or wrong answer. It depends on how you define *creativity*. Pause for a moment and jot down your own definition.

There are many published definitions relating to *creativity*.
- "The power or quality to create rather than imitate."
  (*Merriam-Webster's Collegiate Dictionary*, 10th Edition)

- "Changing things is central to leadership, and changing them before anyone else is creativeness." (Anthony Jay, *Management and Machiavelli*)

- "Every act of creation is first of all an act of destruction." (Picasso)

- "A process that results in novelty, which is accepted as useful, tenable, or satisfying by a significant group of others at some point in time." (Morris Stein)

- "An idea that all experts think is crazy when you propose it, and everyone else thinks is obvious once it's proven." (Daniel Koshland)

- "The capacity to find new and unexpected connections, to voyage freely over the seas, to happen on America when we seek new routes to India." (Lawrence Kubie)

For the purposes of this book, let's define *creativity* as "the generation of novel, useful ideas." Let's define *innovation* as "taking the best ideas to market." Creativity is a personal act, while innovation is often a team effort. Innovation is what we ultimately want to achieve, but it won't occur without the generation of novel, useful ideas.

There is a myth that creativity is limited to a few individuals who are naturally creative. In reality, creativity is a skill. It is a skill that can be learned and applied like any other skill.

Research with fraternal and identical twins supports the view that different abilities to think creatively are not inherited.[2] Thinking and creative thinking are learnable skills like driving a car, swimming, golfing, or knitting. Some people will be better at certain things than others; but given sufficient motivation, instruction, and practice, everyone can raise his or her level of skill.

Chapter IV describes creative-thinking tools, processes, and frameworks that aid in raising a motivated person's skill level.

Valuing Creativity in Problem Solving, Innovation, and Quality Improvement

Creative thinking is particularly important in problem solving and innovation. This chapter discusses the role of creative thinking in these processes and where it fits in quality improvement.

CREATIVE PROBLEM SOLVING

Think of problem solving in the broadest sense, i.e., of an issue that needs new direction in thinking. Hence, the problem could relate to searching for new opportunities or new concepts as well as tackling a near-term need.

Basically, creative problem solving has three steps:

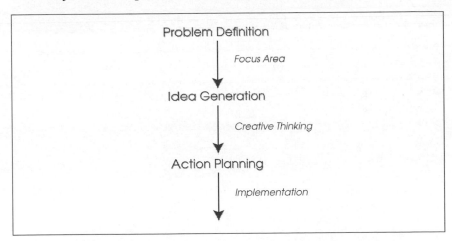

Problem Definition is generally the broad statement of the issue being addressed. To get to the heart of the problem, many possible focus areas are identified, from which three or four are generally selected for the idea-generation step.

Idea Generation is the step where creative thinking is applied to generate many ideas, relative to the focus area, from which the "best" are harvested based on criteria formulated by the group.

Action Planning is the step where plans are formulated to implement the best ideas.

Creative thinking permeates the entire problem-solving process, which often requires stepping outside normal thinking patterns. Creativity techniques are useful not only in the idea-generation step, but throughout the entire process. For example, metaphoric thinking might be used in defining possible focus areas, as illustrated in Chapter IV, Example #10, p. 20. In action planning, creative ideas are usually required to overcome barriers in bringing the idea rapidly to market.

The creative problem-solving process is discussed in greater detail in Chapter IV. Problem-solving workshops are illustrated in Chapter VII, Examples #47–52, pp. 97–101.

INNOVATION

The innovation process has components similar to the creative problem-solving process: definition of a market need; generation of an idea to meet the need; demonstration that the idea meets the need; scale-up; and commercialization, i.e., bringing the idea to reality.

Creative thinking permeates the entire innovation process, similar to the problem-solving process. It is important in identifying needs, in generating productive ideas, and in overcoming barriers to bringing the idea promptly to market.

The innovation process is discussed in greater detail in Chapter IX, which includes a description of five successful innovations and practical learnings from each.

QUALITY IMPROVEMENT

A discussion about how creativity fits with quality improvement led Colonel Rolf Smith, former Director of the Office of Innovation of the United States Air Force, to respond with the concept of Seven Levels of Change.[3]

SEVEN LEVELS OF CHANGE

1. Do Things Right, e.g., follow correct procedures.
2. Do the Right Things, e.g., set priorities.
3. Do Away with Things, e.g., stop doing things that don't count.
4. Do Things Better, e.g., think of ways to continuously improve.
5. Do Things Others Are Doing, e.g. find the best practices.
6. Do Things That Haven't Been Done.
7. Do Things That "Can't" Be Done.

The first five levels of change are important, and they benefit from creative thinking. But they can usually be addressed through normal patterns of thinking. The last two levels of change are more difficult. Approaches to generating ideas at these levels are aided by the creative-thinking tools, processes, and frameworks described in Chapter IV, on pp. 11–57.

The First Dimension: Learning and Applying Creativity Techniques

This chapter describes 18 creativity techniques and 37 examples of practical application. It is not intended as a comprehensive review, but rather a brief description of those techniques found by the author to be the most productive in the workplace.

Additional examples of practical application are described in later chapters. In Chapter VI, Example #44, p. 80, a creative-thinking session generated an idea that revitalized a program that was about to be dropped. It had a $30 million stake. In Chapter VII, Examples #47–52, pp. 97–101, high-stakes creative problem-solving workshops are described where new ideas and concepts led to financial gains and helped shape strategic direction. In Chapter VIII, Examples #56–57, pp. 124–125, describe how creative thinking led to manufacturing annual cost savings of $6 million and $3 million, respectively, plus other benefits.

Creativity techniques can be categorized in many ways. One approach is to organize them into the following three categories, all having value: pattern-breaking tools; idea-collection processes; and focused thinking frameworks.

PATTERN-BREAKING TOOLS

In tackling difficult issues needing new direction in thinking, it is often necessary to break out of our normal thinking patterns, i.e., to break away from the safe cocoon that we have built for ourselves.

Mechanism of Mind[4] by Dr. Edward de Bono, published in 1969, describes the mind as a self-organizing system. As our mind absorbs information and digests experiences, our thinking organizes itself into patterns based on these inputs. Pattern thinking is essential. Otherwise, we would have to rethink each morning whether we put our shoes on before our socks or our socks before our shoes. In problem solving, normal patterns of thinking are valuable. But to solve difficult problems or conceive radically new concepts often requires that we break away from the constraints of pattern thinking.

Breaking away from normal patterns of thinking is more easily said than done. This is illustrated humorously in the movie *Dead Poets Society.* In this movie, Robin Williams, an instructor at a prep school, tells students to tear out introductory pages in their poetry book. Tearing pages from a book goes against the norm. It's humorous to watch the students' shocked faces as they struggle against stepping outside the paradigm that tearing pages from a book is "sinful."

In another scene, Robin Williams demonstrates his approach to looking at the world differently. He tells his students to jump on top of his desk and look around from that vantage point. He comments, "Break out . . . look around you . . . dare to strike out and find new ground!"

We don't have to jump on top of desks or tables to look at the world differently. Sometimes new ideas and concepts emerge serendipitously.

Serendipity

We don't have to rely on serendipity either. There exist deliberate, systematic, proven tools for creative thinking that help us break away from normal thinking patterns. These tools can be learned and applied as can any skill.

The figure on the next page shows six pattern-breaking tools that will be discussed.

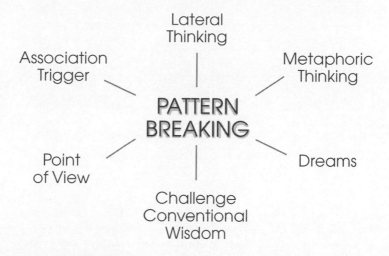

LATERAL THINKING

Perhaps the most productive and easily applied pattern-breaking tool is Dr. Edward de Bono's lateral thinking, described in several of his books.[5-9] Certification courses for training trainers are available.[10]

Lateral thinking is defined in the *Oxford English Dictionary* as:
  "Seeking ways to solve problems by apparently illogical means."

The deliberate tools of Edward de Bono's lateral thinking arise from an understanding of the brain as a self-organizing information system that forms asymmetric patterns. In order to move laterally across these patterns, we need to set up deliberate provocations. We then use the mental operation of movement in order to move on from the provocation. Edward de Bono emphasizes that movement is an active mental operation in which we can become skilled. It is far more than just a suspension of judgment.

In the figure on the next page, visualize tackling a difficult problem and racing "linearly" down a highway going east, the direction of thinking that you perceive might lead to a solution.

DE BONO LATERAL THINKING

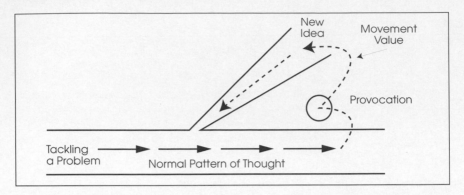

If there is a side road going north, you will likely speed past it, even though it may lead to a wider, faster highway and take you to your destination sooner. There are ways to test these side roads in problem solving or opportunity searching that may lead to better, more novel ideas.

In lateral thinking, the approach taken to test the side roads is to generate *provocations.* These are thoughts related to the issue being tackled, but we know them to be untrue. They are bizarre, impractical, and provocative. The provocation is used for its forward effect—as a stepping stone to shift laterally out of standard, linear patterns of thinking. Think of the provocation as an unstable thought that has no judgment value per se but which, through "movement," leads to new ways to think about the problem. This lateral direction, created by the provocation, is a new starting point at which to address the problem. Lateral thinking will almost always lead to a flow of new, unusual ideas.

Dr. de Bono teaches several techniques that systematically help generate productive provocations:

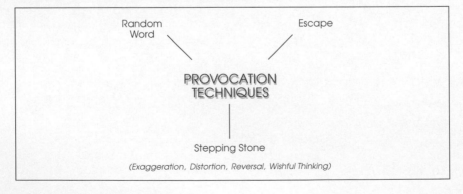

Random word involves creating a new "entry point" by selecting a word at random, e.g., a noun from a dictionary or poster that is not connected to the subject.

Escape involves examining the subject for what we take for granted and then canceling, negating, or escaping from it.

Stepping stone involves the reversal, exaggeration, distortion, or wishful thinking about a subject that is a stepping stone to new ideas.

APPLICATION

The process generally follows three steps:

(1) Selection of a focus area requiring creative new ideas.

(2) Development of provocations relating to the focus area using lateral thinking techniques.

(3) Generation of sensible ideas dealing with the problem, stimulated by the provocations.

The bolder the provocation, the better the chance that it will lead to good, unusual ideas. The challenge is to generate many provocations and ideas until one rings a bell and excites the team. A productive lateral thinking session is one that generates at least one "great" idea worth implementing! The practical application of lateral thinking can best be illustrated by examples.

Example #1

The DuPont Corporate Information Systems group was dealing with this focus area:

How can we reduce costs in the Information Systems function?

This session was led by Nancy McDonald, group manager, who had attended a lateral thinking training workshop. The technique that paid off in this case was *reversal,* which led to the following provocation:

Reduce costs by spending more money.

This provocation generated the idea that spending more money on fewer vendors would provide leverage to obtain large discounts. The approach was to cut the number of vendors and negotiate better prices on high-volume orders. This approach led to an annual savings of over $300,000. Applying this concept to maintenance saved another several hundred thousand dollars annually.

Example #2

An R & D unit made a technical breakthrough that would enable economic manufacture of a proprietary new product. This became a high-priority program with additional resources assigned in engineering, manufacturing, marketing, and business planning. The focus area addressed:

> *How can we move this product to market much faster than the normal development cycle?*

The lateral thinking technique that paid off in this case was *random word*. The word selected at random from a bathing suit advertisement was *beach*. Discussion of *beach* led to a series of thoughts relating to water, to swimming, to swim meets, and to competition. The thought of competition triggered this provocation:

> *Give the breakthrough technology to our toughest competitor.*

This provocative thought focused attention on the company that was the toughest competitor and how they would bring this breakthrough to market.

The toughest competitor in this case was a Japanese company known to move new products to market rapidly. Questioning how they would handle this breakthrough led to an implementation plan with an organizational framework quite different from the prevailing DuPont culture. The plan was accepted by the several functions involved despite the anticipated difficult turf issues. The result was the introduction of the product two to three years faster than normal. This saved millions of dollars in development costs and enabled early assessment of the new technology in the marketplace.

Example #3

A plant technical group was dealing with this focus area:

> *How can we improve continuity of our complex continuous-flow filter system?*

The filter system was based on a reciprocating belt with 70 moving parts that had frequent failures. The group manager, Jean Prideaux, was a creativity champion whose group was educated in lateral thinking. A reversal provocation paid off:

The moving belt is stationary.

This provocation shifted thinking in an entirely new direction and led to the design of a system that reduced the number of moving parts by 80 percent. The result was a major breakthrough in process continuity, product quality, and significant cost savings.

Example #4

A business team had the objective of growing the Lycra® spandex fiber business through identifying additional end use applications. The focus area:

What new end uses can be developed for Lycra®?

The creative-thinking session was facilitated by Gene Pontrelli, a Research Fellow educated in lateral thinking. Several techniques were used to develop provocations. The escape technique paid off. The group listed what they took for granted about Lycra® end uses, e.g., that it was used for stretch apparel, innerwear, womenswear, clothing, people, etc. Escaping from these led to many provocations, one of which was this:

Applications of Lycra® for nonpersons.

This provocation generated ideas such as stretch clothing for dolls, stretch warm-up suits for racehorses, and a new product concept unrelated to textile fabrics or clothing. The latter idea materialized into a program to develop a proprietary new product.

Example #5

The Nomex® plant technical group, working jointly with manufacturing and the engineering department, had developed a prototype for a new computer system for the plant. They were at the stage of purchasing and installing plant-scale equipment. The focus area:

How can we install the computer system in the plant much faster and at a substantially lower cost than forecasted?

The group manager, Ben Jones, was a student of lateral thinking, and he set up a creative-thinking session that included technical, manufacturing, and engineering people. The pay-off provocation was an exaggeration:

Eliminate the engineering department.

This exaggeration stimulated the group to modify the standard approach of preassembling hardware and staging software at the engineering development facilities before shipping the system to the plant. They decided to take the risk of eliminating this step entirely. The approach was to have the engineering department team, working with manufacturing and technical, integrate the new computer system directly into the plant process. This approach succeeded, saving well over $1 million in development costs and accelerating installation an estimated one to two years. This example became a model for value partnering among functions.

Example #6

A group of lawyers requested a creative-thinking session to deal with the issue:

How can we spend less time in meetings?

Lateral thinking was explained by master facilitator Charlie Prather and applied to this issue. The random word *rest room* led one participant to comment that when he goes to the rest room, he does what he has to do and then leaves. This led to the idea that they should each agree to remain in a meeting only as long as the subject is pertinent to their work. Normally, they had been remaining for entire meetings out of courtesy to the speakers, but they had been wasting much time. A side benefit was that speakers would pay more attention to addressing topics that were pertinent to the audience.

Example #7

A seminar for high school students was held to introduce them to creative-thinking skills. To illustrate lateral thinking, the focus area selected was:

How can we make learning in the classroom more fun?

Many provocations were developed using lateral thinking tools. Wishful thinking led to this provocation:

Eliminate the need for teachers.

This provocation led to the idea that once a month, a student or team of students would take turns conducting the lesson, and the teacher would become part of the student group. Some of the teachers in the audience said they would implement this idea.

Example #8

A two-hour session was held with a group of about 20 schoolteachers. They addressed this issue:

> *How can we overcome barriers to learning in the classroom?*

Lateral thinking was explained, and many ideas were generated. The random word *supermarket* paid off. It produced the concept that when people go shopping in a supermarket, they have a host of products to choose from. This led to the idea that at the beginning of the term, the teacher would develop a menu of topics he or she planned to cover. The students would then prioritize the list according to the topics they were most interested in learning about. The teachers evaluated and upgraded this idea using the de Bono Six Thinking Hats framework described later in this chapter. Some of the teachers were enthusiastic about implementing the concept during the next school year.

General Comments

In general, lateral thinking sessions tackling difficult issues take several hours. Many provocations are generated and pursued before one precipitates an idea that the group is excited about pursuing. Sometimes there is overlap in the provocation techniques, but that is not important. What is important is the development of bold provocations that might lead to useful new ideas.

While group thinking is beneficial, the techniques can also be used by an individual. The lateral thinking described in Example #2, p. 16, was done by an individual who was contemplating the issue while returning from a quality leadership conference.

METAPHORIC THINKING

> *I try to think like nature to find the right questions. You don't invent the answers, you reveal the answers from nature. In nature, the answers to our problems already exist. Think like nature. Ask "How would nature solve this problem?"*
>
> Dr. Jonas Salk

Metaphoric thinking is a powerful creative-thinking tool. New ideas are generated by connecting the problem under attack to something that occurs in a totally unrelated system, often in nature.

Many books and articles have been written about metaphoric thinking and how it relates to learning, knowing, and problem solving.[2, 12–14] This section illustrates its value in problem solving.

Example #9

This example illustrates how a researcher used metaphoric thinking to solve a difficult technical problem, where others before him had failed.

Nomex® aramid fiber is inherently flame-resistant and used in applications such as protective clothing, electrical insulation, and honeycomb aircraft panels. To expand Nomex® markets into flame-resistant fabrics for drapes, upholstery and carpets, a need existed to develop a product that could be dyed in customers' mills without special procedures. Many research programs failed to accomplish this objective, because it was difficult for dyes to penetrate the tight Nomex® fiber structure unless chemical swelling agents were used in customer plants. These agents caused serious waste-disposal problems.

A research scientist, Eric Vance, working on the Nomex® dyeing problem at the DuPont Pioneering Research Laboratory, used metaphoric thinking. He asked himself, "What in nature has a tight structure but can be penetrated—and how?" His answer: the earth! For example, we build coal mines by digging a tunnel using structure props. This prevents the dug-out hole from collapsing, allowing miners to enter.

Vance applied the earth metaphor to the Nomex® problem. He imbibed a large organic molecule into the fiber structure during manufacture. This molecule propped open the structure and allowed entrance of dyes under standard mill-dyeing conditions. The dye entered, the props collapsed, and the dyes stayed in the fiber.

Today, a dyeable, flame-resistant Nomex®, trademarked Colorguard®, is used in many commercial applications including colorful airplane interiors that have to satisfy FAA flammability regulations.

Example #10

Metaphoric thinking can be used in creative problem-solving sessions to define potential focus areas.

A business unit was losing money and held a problem-solving session to generate ideas on how to reduce costs in the manufacturing process. Master Facilitator Mary Roush cast the participants as a group of physicians, e.g., a cardiologist, a neurologist, and so on, who had a critically ill patient to treat. The patient was the metaphor for the problem they were working on. They examined the patient for vital signs such as heart failure, waste elimination, and mental problems. This approach led to defining many potential treatment protocols that could be followed to help the patient regain health. For example, a heart transplant would mean replacing outdated vital equipment in the plant. This approach led to many possible focus areas, which served as the basis for the rest of the problem-solving session discussed in Example #48, p. 98.

Example #11

A special task force was addressing the problem of how to reduce dust in their manufacturing plant. They developed a long list of ideas using normal thinking patterns, but none were very good. After switching to metaphoric thinking, they considered how nature removes dust from the environment. One way that nature removes dust is by heavy rainfall. This thought shifted their thinking to an entirely new direction that led to an elegant but simple way to remove dust in their operation.

Example #12

A human resources group used metaphoric thinking to generate fresh ideas for enhancing recruitment success. The following metaphors led to many good ideas:
- Recruitment is like choosing a partner or spouse.
- Recruitment is like fishing.
- Recruitment is like growing a garden.

Example #13

Metaphoric thinking can aid in the communication of a concept.

A colleague was distraught because he felt he had lost his effectiveness as a trainer. He had been the trainer in a particular business unit, but the organization had been restructured, and he was now part of a new centralized training unit. His problem was that whereas in the past he had been an insider to one business unit, he now felt like an outsider to two new business units. He was having difficulty understanding the concept of centralization and how he might be effective in his new role.

A metaphor immediately clarified his understanding. It was suggested that he view the new organizational structure as a three-ring circus. He had the opportunity to be an insider in each of the three rings. In one ring, he would be part of the centralized group sharing learnings about training. At other times, he would be inside one of the other two rings as the trainer for that business unit. This metaphor helped him understand how he would operate, and he regained his confidence.

CAPTURING & INTERPRETING DREAMS

When and how my dreams come, I know not, nor can I force them. Those pleasures that please me I retain in memory and am accustomed, as I have been told, to hum them to myself. If I continue in this way, it soon occurs to me how I may turn this or that morsel to account so as to make a good dish of it . . . All this fires my soul, and . . . my subject enlarges itself and becomes methodised and defined, and the whole, though it be long, stands almost complete and finished in my mind so I can survey it like a fine statue or a beautiful picture, at a glance . . . All this inventing, this producing, takes place in a pleasing, lively dream.

Wolfgang Amadeus Mozart

Capturing and interpreting dreams is a technique for harnessing the subconscious. It is a way to help seed new ideas, solve problems and envision new opportunities.

Have you ever experienced going to sleep with a problem and waking up the next morning with a clearer view of the problem and new approaches to solving it? This happens because the mind continues to function while we sleep. In the subconscious state, the mind is less inhibited.

Donald MacKinnon writes about the contribution of Sigmund Freud to our understanding of human nature and the role of the unconscious mental process:

Freud saw human nature as deeply conflicted and considered conflict to be the source of creativity as well as neurosis, and the creative process related to dreaming.[17]

MacKinnon writes that while Freud stressed the role of the repressed unconscious processes in creativity, later investigators, such as Kubie in 1961, have argued that an even more crucial and more positive role is played by the preconscious:

> *The preconscious involves processes which, though not conscious at the moment, may readily become so; the sum total of all things which we know and which we can recall, but of which we are not conscious of at the moment. The preconscious is a fluid reservoir of images, ideas, and memories that easily interact with one another to form new combinations . . . It is in the preconscious that creative imagination and the illuminating flash of insight occur.*

Ned Herrmann's Applied Creative Thinking Workshop, described in Chapter V, teaches keeping a pad and pencil at bedside to record dreams immediately after awakening. Otherwise, dreams are quickly forgotten. Once in hand, dreams can be interpreted relative to the problem on the person's mind the night before.

Example #14

The dream technique helped solve a difficult plant equipment problem. The "creative dreamer" was Floyd Ragsdale, a manufacturing team member fighting the problem. In his words:

> *We had been fighting collapsing vacuum hoses in the Kevlar® process for months. It was taking a tremendous toll on our yields. One day, I had been at the plant trying to find a solution for maybe 16 hours, and I needed some sleep. When I went home and got into bed, the problem throbbed in my head like a toothache. Back and forth, back and forth. Eventually, I fell asleep. I started to dream . . . and in my dreams, I saw slinky toys, those spring-like coils that kids play with. I kept seeing these toy-like springs over and over.*

> *I had been to a creativity workshop at the plant only a month before. One of the lessons was that we should pay attention to our dreams, because sometimes we have better insights when we relax and don't concentrate so hard. So I kept a pad and paper next to my bed. I came out of my dream and sat up. Still half asleep, I wrote on the pad: "Insert spring inside of vacuum hose, will correct problem." Then I went back to sleep. When I woke up about 4:30 or 5:00 and headed into the plant, I took my paper with me. I saw the area supervisor and said, "We're in luck. I had a dream. Our problem is solved." He looked at me kind of funny, but I explained, and we ordered some customized stainless steel springs and inserted them in the hose. Doggone, that equipment started up running like a top and has been running well ever since.*

Some people have wondered why the plant team had not thought about a spring sooner, it seemed so obvious. As Edward de Bono writes, "Most good ideas are obvious in hindsight." How often has someone come up with a good idea and you wondered why that hadn't been thought of before? It's like climbing a mountain and not seeing the best path up until reaching the top and looking down. The good idea may seem obvious in hindsight, but it wasn't to the people while they were "climbing that mountain."

Example #15

This example illustrates how a dream can influence a person's direction in thinking.

In 1986, the author attended the Ned Herrmann Applied Creative Thinking Workshop (Chapter V), which requires participants to bring with them a problem they are dealing with at home or at work. The author selected: "How can I enhance the environment for creativity and innovation in my organization?" Exercises during the week helped attendees spend quality time in several ways thinking about their elected problem. This set the stage to experience "dreaming" a solution to the problem.

Toward the end of the week, participants were directed to go to their sleeping quarters, lie down, and put on a set of headphones. A pencil and pad was at bedside to record dreams. A sleep-inducing narrative was played to lull everyone into the "creative" theta state. Some people fell asleep and couldn't remember any dreams. The author had a snapshot dream. He saw row after row of tied hands held high above people's heads. At first, he did not know how to interpret this dream. Then it struck him. To enhance the environment for creativity and innovation, he should "untie the hands" of employees. He should enable more space and freedom to generate new ideas, take risks, and try new things. Hence, this dream was an important influence on his direction in thinking and management style.

Example #16

Designing problem-solving workshops with an evening between sessions enables participants to return the next morning and describe dreams they may have had. The group can then attempt to interpret the dreams, which might provide new approaches to the problem.

A business unit was dealing with the issue of ways to improve delivery time of their products from the plant to the customer. Many ideas were generated in the problem-solving session using pattern thinking and various creativity tools. By the end of the day, everyone was steeped in the problem. At that point, the facilitator described the value of dreams tapping the subconscious and suggested that they record any dreams they might have that night.

The next morning, one of the participants described a dream in which her boss was running amok in the plant. This was atypical of him. The group's interpretation of this dream was that the plant was in a serious crisis. If they didn't at least double the speed of delivery, the plant would shut down, and they would lose their jobs! This stimulated the group to shift gears into "crisis thinking." This type of thinking increased the intensity of the meeting and unleashed a swarm of more radical ideas, some judged to be worth implementing.

CHALLENGING CONVENTIONAL WISDOM

When a distinguished but elderly scientist states that something is possible, he is almost always certainly right. When he states something is impossible, he is very probably wrong.

Tom Alexandra, *The Wild Birds Find a Corporate Roost*

Challenging conventional wisdom is the deliberate questioning of existing paradigms and a willingness to take risks to buck the tide of popular opinion. This characteristic comes naturally to many scientific researchers.

The three examples described below illustrate how challenging conventional wisdom led to the Kevlar® aramid fiber venture. Kevlar® applications include bullet-resistant vests, fireblocking fabrics, and reinforcement of tires, brake linings, and high-performance composites in aircraft.

Example #17

In the early 1960s, the DuPont Pioneering Research Laboratory management had a vision for a super fiber with the heat resistance of asbestos and the stiffness of glass. The breakthrough occurred in 1965, when research scientist Stephanie Kwolek prepared a solution of an opaque aromatic polyamide polymer that could not be clarified by heating or filtration. This implied that inert matter was dispersed in the solution, which would plug the spinneret holes and prevent spinning into fibers. Furthermore, the solution viscosity was too low and could not possibly be fiber-forming. The experienced spinning technician refused to spin it.

Kwolek bucked conventional wisdom. She insisted on attempting to extrude the opaque, watery solution. Surprisingly, it spun well. We now know that the opacity was due to the formation of polymer liquid crystals that shear-oriented in the spinneret capillaries, yielding well-formed fibers. This scientific discovery was the basis of what later became Kevlar®, an aramid fiber that has five times the strength of steel at equal weight. This discovery also catalyzed an entirely new field of scientific research.

Example #18

Following Kwolek's discovery, another major breakthrough was required to achieve a practical scale-up process. The spinning solvent had to be 100 percent sulfuric acid, a very viscous solution that limited the polymer concentration and spinning throughputs necessary for an economic process. The lab "wisdom" was that the solution couldn't be heated because the sulfuric acid would degrade the polymer. Herb Blades, Engineering Fellow, challenged conventional wisdom and heated the solution to elevated temperatures. This led to a major breakthrough, since under these conditions, the polymer did not degrade, but unexpectedly formed a crystalline complex with the sulfuric acid. This enabled spinning at much higher polymer concentrations than previously possible and dramatically improved spinning economics.

Example #19

Another difficult challenge in the Kevlar® development was to demonstrate the market potential for this unique fiber that would not fit into conventional fiber applications. The high modulus and thermal stability of Kevlar® led to its consideration as an asbestos replacement in brakes and other rubber-reinforcement applications. This was quickly ruled out by most experts, because asbestos was cheap and Kevlar® was very expensive. However, two researchers bucked conventional thinking. They converted Kevlar® into very short fibers, called "pulp," and found that only 1 percent of this new fiber form, uniformly dispersed in the base matrix, would provide reinforcement equivalent to over 50 percent of asbestos. This discovery opened the door to major markets for Kevlar®, which has replaced asbestos in most truck brake linings, gaskets, and in many other applications.

The Kevlar® innovation is discussed in greater detail in Chapter IX, "Taking Ideas to Market."

POINT OF VIEW

Changing our point of view about an issue, an event, or a thing can jog our thinking outside normal patterns and lead to entirely new ideas and concepts. Positive thinking, substitution, and fantasizing are tools to help change point of view.

Positive Thinking

Positive thinking involves viewing a negative from different angles and turning it into a positive.

A story about two shoe companies illustrates what we mean by *positive thinking.* Each company sent a representative to a developing country to help decide whether to build a shoe factory. The first representative wired back, "Nobody wears shoes here, don't build factory." The second representative wired back, "NOBODY WEARS SHOES HERE . . . OPPORTUNITY UNLIMITED . . . BUILD LARGE FACTORY!"

Turn Failures into Successes—Think Positively!

Example #20

A major carpet product (now commercial) was the result of a research scientist turning a negative into a positive.

A need existed for a more rapidly dyeable nylon fiber. Israel David, research scientist at the DuPont Experimental Station, took the approach to chemically modify the nylon. In one experiment, the result was the opposite of what he expected or wanted. The fiber could not be dyed at all! Instead of viewing this as a negative result, he took a positive view. He reasoned that he could mix this nondyeable fiber with dyeable fibers and get unique styling effects. This was the birth of dye-resistant styling yarns, which materialized into a profitable product in the nylon carpet line.

Example #21

Sometimes, what seems like a serious reversal turns out to be a blessing in disguise.

A task force was formed to plan an Innovator Forum, a major DuPont conference illustrating the value of innovation in company growth. Several intensive months were spent collecting examples of successful innovations worldwide, screening abstracts of potential speakers, enlisting keynote speakers, contracting facilities, designing and purchasing awards, and organizing the agenda for the three-day conference. Two weeks before the conference, top management unexpectedly canceled all meetings, including the Innovator Forum, to conserve cash.

The task team was at first demoralized by the negative turn of events. However, they decided to think positively about how to capitalize on the work already done. The result was a creative plan that had greater impact than would have been possible had the conference been held. An agreement was reached that, instead of a single corporate event, all sites would hold a local event where the site innovators would present their talks and receive the awards. This approach was not only more cost-effective, but it exposed a much larger number of employees to the innovation theme. Another outcome was the publication of seven bound reports containing the innovation examples that were widely distributed. The Innovator Forum is discussed in greater detail in Chapter VII.

Substitution

A technique taught by Roger von Oech is to substitute your own thinking with the point of view of another person known for having a unique style of problem solving. The approach is to ask, "What if so-and-so had this problem? How would he or she attack it?" Examples of such people include Walt Disney, Lee Iacocca, Marie Curie, George Patton, Pablo Picasso, Ronald Reagan, Winston Churchill, Joseph Stalin, Rosabeth Kanter, Albert Einstein, Sigmund Freud, George Burns, Vince Lombardi, your nine-year-old son, your spouse.

Example #22

A business unit was searching for ideas for how to cut through red tape and commercialize a new product rapidly. The technique that proved the most useful was to view the problem from the point of view of Lee Iacocca.

Someone in the group related a story he had heard about how Iacocca reentered Chrysler into the convertible automobile market. At the time, convertibles had been out of style for years because of safety issues. Iacocca decided to test the public reaction to a convertible and asked his manufacturing manager how fast he could deliver a convertible to display. The response was that, given special priority, it could be ready in about six months. As the story goes, Iacocca turned red with anger. He ordered the manager to rip off the roof of an existing car and have the convertible ready the next morning.

The above story lifted the business team to a more intensive plateau of creative thinking. There was a burst of aggressive, unorthodox ideas, in tune with how Iacocca would approach their problem, e.g., elimination of all paperwork. This paid off and helped lay the basis of a fast-track program.

Fantasizing

A technique taught by Joyce Juntune and Morris Stein is to think outside normal patterns. They suggest changing your point of view about an object by first eyeing it analytically and then by fantasizing.

Example #23

Select a pencil and describe it from an analytical point of view. For example, it might be round, yellow, eight inches long, have a gray lead point and a half-worn eraser. Now fantasize. For example, I wish that it could do the following: write by itself; be eaten; never wear out; sharpen itself; write in several colors; and illuminate the darkness. Using this technique with a team of three or four diverse thinkers would likely generate, within 30 minutes, over 100 ideas from which some could be selected to form the basis for a new line of pencils.

ASSOCIATION TRIGGER

Association trigger is making an observation about an object, event or thought associated with a need that might trigger a new idea on how to meet that need. It involves having a "prepared mind," being aware of needs, and being alert to unexpected signals that might provide a new approach to meet the need.

Example #24

The following example illustrates how a major business venture was born by a researcher observing an unusual phenomenon that he associated with a need, triggering an idea to meet the need.

George Kinney, a research engineer at the DuPont Experimental Station, was exploring ways to spin a fuzzy nylon filament yarn. His approach was to blow short floc fibers against a molten spinning threadline to obtain hair-like projections. He couldn't get the floc fibers to stick, so he tried electrostatics. As the yarn fell to the floor, the electrostatically charged fibers spread out into a sheet-like structure. At the time (mid-1950s), there was a need in the marketplace for low-cost nonwoven fabrics from synthetic fibers. Kinney was aware of this need (he had a "prepared mind"). His observation of the fibers spreading into a sheet on the floor triggered an entirely new concept in sheet-structure formation. This observation ultimately led to the DuPont Reemay® and Typar® spunbonded nonwoven fabric businesses.

Example #25

This example illustrates how a phrase in an aims statement triggered an idea that led to an effective way to communicate concepts in creativity and innovation.

The DuPont OZ Creative Thinking Network described in Chapter VII had an objective to engage employees company-wide in the field of creative thinking. A phrase in the OZ aims statement "to function as a creativity network in a way that is . . . fun rather than drudgery" triggered OZ member Fred Dickson to think about cartoons as an engaging way to communicate concepts in creativity and innovation. The triggered idea activated a project that materialized into a copyrighted cartoon book entitled *Are We Creative Yet?*[18] This book contains essays by DuPont employees, paired with cartoons by Bob Thaves, that make serious points about creativity with a light touch. Ed Woolard, Chairman of the

DuPont company, wrote the foreword. Over 20,000 copies of this book have been sold or donated to educators.

The OZ Creative Thinking Network and the story of how the cartoon book idea was taken to market is described in Chapter VII.

IDEA-COLLECTION PROCESSES

There are many processes that help collect and organize ideas generated within normal thinking patterns. In problem-solving sessions, it is best to start with some of these processes. When teams have exhausted ideas generated within normal thinking patterns, then pattern-breaking techniques such as lateral thinking and metaphoric thinking, discussed in the previous section, help trigger a flow of new, more unusual, creative ideas. This section highlights some idea-collection processes:

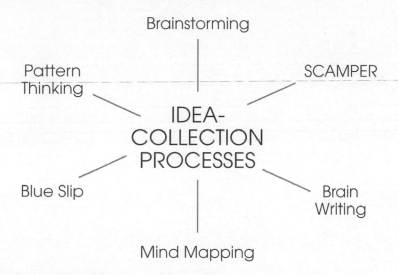

BRAINSTORMING

In 1938, Alex Osborn first employed organized ideation in the company he then headed.[19] The early participants dubbed their efforts "Brainstorm Sessions," because they were using their brains to storm a problem. Brainstorming became popular worldwide. It is defined in *Merriam Webster's Collegiate Dictionary*, 10th Edition, as:

> *A group problem-solving technique that involves the spontaneous contribution of ideas from all members of the group.*

Dr. Osborn points out in his book that this type of conference was not entirely new. A similar procedure has been used in India for more than 400 years by Hindu teachers while working with religious groups. The Indian name for this method is Prai-Barshana. In such a session there is no discussion or criticism. Evaluation of ideas takes place at later meetings of the same group.

Modern brainstorming is usually part of a problem-solving session in which a checklist of ideas is generated that leads to problem solution. The objective is to collect, usually on hang charts, a large quantity of ideas. Building on others' ideas is encouraged. The deferment-of-judgment principle is strictly followed. The ideas are subsequently evaluated and processed.

A brainstorming warm-up helps create an environment and mind frame conducive to an uninhibited free-flow of ideas. An effective, enjoyable technique is used by members of the Center for Studies in Creativity at Buffalo State College. In this technique, the facilitators use a five-minute brainstorming exercise that asks teams to think of 50–100 ideas on how to modify a bathtub. The teams are generally able to do this. Then the facilitators unexpectedly ask teams for an additional 50–100 bathtub ideas, which is more difficult. The teams find, to their surprise, that they are able to do this. By the time the participants complete this exercise, they have lost their mental inhibitions and are ready to brainstorm the problem at hand. The Buffalo group has an excellent process for harvesting the best ideas using an interactive criteria-setting technique.[24]

MIND MAPPING

Mind mapping is a process originated by Tony Buzan that combines right-brain generation of ideas with left-brain organization of those ideas around a central theme. In contrast with traditional listing of ideas or thoughts down a page, mind mapping places the core subject in the center of the page as a starting point for generation of multiple ideas that branch out in many directions. Mind mapping has many applications, including note taking, organizing presentations, and problem solving. It is a productive aid to group or individual brainstorming.

Mind mapping laws, including the use of color and images, are listed in Tony Buzan's book.[20] In practice, there are many variations depending on individual preferences. Joyce Wycoff's workbook provides an excellent overview of mind mapping and an approach to practical applications.[21]

Example #26

A mind map helped organize this chapter:

BLUE SLIP

This technique involves writing ideas on 4" x 3" blue slips, usually in response to thought-provoking questions. Each slip has a subject title at the top and one idea. The blue-slip process is taught by Dale Clawson and Rolf Smith, former Directors, Office of Innovation, United States Air Force. It is an excellent way to collect and assemble ideas generated by a group, and to record and save one's own ideas on an ongoing basis.

Example #27

The blue-slip process was applied in a meeting of technical managers to identify ways to improve functional effectiveness.

The four questions asked, suggested by Rolf Smith:
- If you could be in charge for a year, what would you change?
- What prevents you from doing your job better?
- What can we stop doing?
- What should we not tamper with?

Participants wrote down their thoughts on many blue slips as each question was asked. The slips were collected and summarized, and the ideas were used as a basis for discussion at the next technical function meeting, where an action plan was formulated.

SCAMPER

This technique provides a checklist of seven verbs to systematically stimulate ideas:

Substitute, Combine, Adapt, Modify, Put to other uses, Eliminate, Rearrange.[22]

SCAMPER is sometimes used in classroom work to help students generate ideas about a subject. For example, Ronni Cohen, elementary school teacher and winner of the 1994 National Entrepreneurship Educator of the Year Award, has applied this technique in the classroom to generate ideas about how to invent new products. She illustrated the process in a monthly meeting of the Creative Educator Network of Delaware by having the group apply SCAMPER to creatively design a modernistic briefcase for the 21st century. Within ten minutes, teams developed many interesting new concepts for a briefcase.

BRAIN WRITING

This technique has members of a problem-solving team silently build on each other's ideas. It is a way to collect ideas from less vocal team members.

The process starts with one participant listing three ideas related to the problem across the top of a sheet of paper. The sheet is then placed in the center of the table. Another team member picks up this sheet and adds his or her ideas, stimulated by the other persons' ideas. This continues until the sheets of paper are filled. The facilitator then posts these sheets on hang charts for future processing along with other ideas generated during the problem-solving session.

PATTERN THINKING

It is the most basic of the idea-collection processes. *Pattern thinking* involves bringing to bear a person's best thinking on how to solve a problem based on his or her knowledge and experience. It differs from brainstorming in that the focus in pattern thinking is on quality rather than quantity.

Pattern thinking is a good way to begin the idea-generation step in creative problem solving. It provides time for participants to discuss their best ideas within their normal experience base. This step might take as long as an hour as participants share their thinking on the problem. These ideas are captured on hang charts as part of the total pool of ideas collected during the session.

In harvesting best ideas, some that were collected during pattern thinking are often among the best ideas considered for action planning.

FOCUSED THINKING FRAMEWORKS

The quality of our thinking will determine the quality of our future.

Edward de Bono

Focused thinking frameworks play a vital role in structuring the approach to problem solving, opportunity searching, and creatively organizing one's thoughts around a subject or issue. This section describes six productive frameworks for focused thinking.

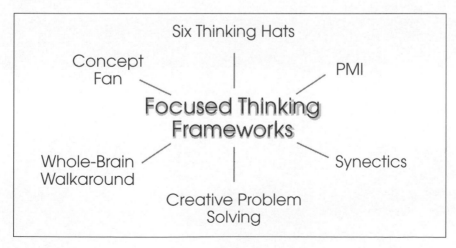

THE SIX THINKING HATS

The Six Thinking Hats,[23] designed by Dr. Edward de Bono, is an ingenious framework to think through a subject in a focused way that makes time and space for creative thinking. It is used extensively in companies such as DuPont, IBM, Prudential Life Insurance, British Airways, Siemens, and Statoil (Norway) to have efficient, productive meetings. Some of these organizations have reported that use of the Six Hats can reduce meeting times to one quarter of what they have been.

Research by John Culvenor at Ballarat University (Australia) has shown that safety engineers trained in the six hats produced more and better ideas and were also better able to prioritize and assess ideas. Indeed one person trained in the hats was more productive than three engineers who had not been trained. In a recent experiment with 300 senior public servants, the use of the hats increased the thinking productivity five-fold.

This section briefly overviews the Six Thinking Hats framework, and describes practical applications. A thorough treatment is in Dr. de Bono's book. Certification courses for training of trainers are available.[10]

Overview

The underlying principle in the Six Thinking Hats framework is that parallel thinking is more productive than argument. There are six hats. Each hat has a different color and represents a different dimension in thinking about the subject being addressed. Everyone wears the same hat at the same time. The hats can be put on and taken off depending on the sequence of thinking that makes the most sense. The six hats and main focus of each is shown below:

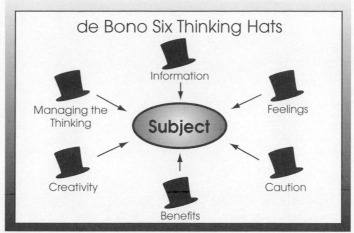

© The McQuaig Group Inc.

The Six Thinking Hats framework is easily explained to participants by an experienced facilitator in 10–15 minutes and can effectively help people think through difficult issues in one to two hours. It encourages parallel thinking with others, directs thinking in discrete segments, switches thinking from one mode to another, separates ego from performance, and provides a way to systematically explore a subject thoroughly and creatively. It can be used individually or in groups, at work or at home.

Practical Applications

The Six Thinking Hats framework is a powerful tool for focused thinking in meetings and also has value as a personal checklist in thinking about a subject. Applications include the following: evaluating and upgrading ideas and concepts; evaluating proposals; resolving controversial issues while gaining buy-in; generating new ideas and concepts; planning for implementation of an idea; and constructively critiquing meetings, seminars, and workshops.

Evaluating and Upgrading Ideas and Concepts

The six-hat process is often applied in creative-thinking sessions to evaluate and upgrade ideas that have been collected during the idea-generation phase. Another value of the process is to provide a mechanism for thoroughly inspecting and upgrading new concepts before taking action.

Example #28

A food company was dealing with the issue of how they might improve competitive position in home delivery of their food products. The facilitator led a group of 12 participants through an idea-generation process that provided many ideas using creativity tools such as lateral thinking. The ideas were posted on flip charts. From this list, the group selected the three ideas they perceived to be the best for further evaluation and upgrading. The facilitator then overviewed the Six Thinking Hats framework, which they applied to each of the selected ideas. The sequence began with yellow hat thinking to define benefits that helped reinforce the idea. Black hat thinking focused attention on difficulties and barriers that would have to be overcome. Green hat thinking led to creative ways to overcome the barriers. White hat thinking identified information needed to fill gaps in their knowledge base and to implement the idea. They followed this sequence for each of the selected ideas. Then each participant did red hat thinking to express their feelings about which idea to carry forward to action planning. This two-hour session provided the group manager with three well-thought-through options available to increasing competitive position and helped decide on resource allocation priorities.

Example #29

A high-technology company embarked upon a program to develop a next-generation process to produce its bread-and-butter product. A task force was formed that spent several weeks identifying three alternative approaches. The task force manager scheduled a one-day creative-thinking session with the objective of creatively upgrading and evaluating each approach as input on resource allocation.

The Six Thinking Hats framework was ideally suited to accomplish the session objectives. The group was organized into three six-member teams. Each team was assigned one of the identified approaches to a next-generation process. The task force manager introduced the meeting objectives and led an interactive discussion on information available on each of the three approaches. The facilitator overviewed the six-hat framework. The teams then applied the six-hat framework, with the aid of the facilitator, to their assigned next-generation process.

Each team started with yellow hat thinking to define the benefits of the approach they were assigned to and why it was feasible. This was followed by black hat thinking to critically review barriers, from which the team selected the three most important. The next step was green hat thinking, where each team developed many ideas on how to overcome the barriers. The ideas were developed by first using normal patterns of thinking. The facilitator then introduced pattern-breaking tools described earlier in this chapter, which stimulated a host of additional ideas, many of which were more unusual than the previous ones.

Each team harvested three to six best ideas by red hat thinking. They then reexamined the next-generation process they were dealing with and upgraded it using input from green hat thinking. Finally, white hat thinking defined what information would be needed to fill gaps in their knowledge and to implement the upgraded next-generation process.

At several points in the workshop, each team shared its thinking with the entire group to benefit from proposed actions and each other's views. As a final step, each team leader summarized team output, including ways to upgrade the next-generation process they were working with. Particularly productive was the sharing of ideas on ways to upgrade the basic concept of each approach being considered. This blue hat phase of the meeting helped build consensus on the task ahead and provided the task force manager with information he needed to decide on a path forward.

Evaluating Proposals

When evaluating a proposal, it's often best to begin with white hat thinking to provide a sound understanding of what is being proposed. This lays the groundwork for next steps in the six-hat framework, where participants judging the proposal can think it through interactively before deciding on whether to proceed. Green hat thinking provides the opportunity to modify the proposal, which helps gain support and buy-in.

Gathering Information

FRANK AND ERNEST ©by Bob Thaves

Example #30

The following example illustrates the value of taking the time to think through a proposal in a structured way before initiating a program that could lead to a waste of resources.

A corporate advisory committee of eight senior executives were asked to consider a proposal that all Research and Development Directors submit a structured cost-benefit analysis on each of their major programs. This would help decide annual budget allocations. The proposal submitted in writing was well-received and supported by most members of the committee.

The Committee Chairman was familiar with the Six Thinking Hats framework and asked an internal facilitator, experienced in the six-hat process, to design a one-hour meeting to resolve this issue.

The meeting began with a brief overview by the facilitator of the Six Thinking Hats framework. The overview was followed by a review of the specific proposal by one of its champions. Yellow hat thinking generated a long list of benefits. It appeared obvious that the proposal should be implemented. However, it turned out otherwise!

When the group interacted in black hat thinking, many serious negatives emerged, such as credibility of cost-benefit assumptions. While green hat thinking generated many ideas for upgrading the proposal to overcome obstacles, none were convincing. The Committee decided against the proposal.

Example #31

This example relates to focused thinking about a family issue.

A son graduating college as a finance major decided that instead of looking for a job he wanted to start his own business. He approached his dad to propose purchasing a franchise business. What particularly caught the father's attention was the son's comment that he was going to ask him to finance the venture. The father suggested that they think the proposal through using the Six Thinking Hats, which the son was familiar with.

Under the white hat, the son described information he had about the franchise. In yellow hat thinking, the son had many points to make regarding benefits. As the father became more acquainted with the prospects, he enthusiastically joined in with additional values to the proposal. During black hat thinking, the mother became part of the group. This was beneficial, since critical thinking came easily for her.

In this session, the white hat was quite valuable. The family returned to the white hat thinking toward the end of the discussion. They focused in parallel on what additional information would be needed before a decision could be reached. This became the basis for action steps. Guess what the family used as the focal point in green hat thinking: *What alternatives are available to finance the project?*

The entire session took about 45 minutes to think through the proposal, generate action steps, and gain buy-in of the parents, who wound up financing the project.

Resolving Controversial Issues and Gaining Buy-In

The Six Thinking Hats framework helps resolve controversial issues in a way that usually gains buy-in of parties on both sides of the issue.

Example #32

This example illustrates the value of sometimes reversing the usual sequence of hats, e.g., doing black hat thinking before yellow hat thinking.

Black Hat Thinking

FRANK & ERNEST® by Bob Thaves

A strategic planning team in an R & D division supporting a portfolio of business units developed a concept that could lead to a profitable new business. The new business would broaden the portfolio, which would capitalize on the strengths of existing businesses. The concept was controversial. The business managers felt that the plan would dilute resources from their businesses, and they strongly opposed the proposal. The R & D management was strongly in favor of the plan. Upper management scheduled a two-hour meeting to resolve the issue. The R & D team designed the meeting based on the Six Thinking Hats framework, which was familiar to the group.

The meeting started with a brief white hat overview of the concept and a discussion to clarify the proposal. Then, instead of yellow hat thinking to elucidate benefits, the facilitator had everyone put on the black hat. This created an energetic discussion among the business managers, which resulted in many hang charts listing serious difficulties inherent in the concept. This approach allowed the business managers to air all the reasons, many justified, why they were opposed to expanding the portfolio with this new business.

The facilitator then had everyone switch to yellow hat thinking. There was dead silence. The R & D people purposely said nothing. Then one of the business managers noted a benefit. Then another business manager noted another benefit. Within 15 minutes, all the business managers joined in, and there were as many hang charts on benefits as there were on difficulties.

Next, the facilitator moved to the green hat to generate ideas on how to retain the benefits while overcoming the difficulties. By this time, everyone was energetically generating ideas to upgrade the proposed concept to make it workable.

The outcome was that the R & D team was charged to develop an implementation plan for further review embodying the changes suggested by the business managers who now had strong buy-in.

Example #33

This example appeared in a Fletcher Challenge Building Products Sector internal publication featuring the status of their creative-thinking effort:

> *Assistant Branch Manager Peter Perry, who facilitated three half-day sessions related to introducing team selling, believes the Six Thinking Hats technique removed most of the conflict from the proposal to shift from individual to team-based commissions in the interest of better customer service.*

> *A lot of people were affected by the change, and there were some strong reservations about it. The Six Thinking Hats let us look at the positives and negatives and helped us define our ideas to put before management, which they in turn modified and sent back to us. If we hadn't used the technique, it's likely there would have been much more resistance to the change and some casualties in terms of losing good stuff.*

Generating New Ideas and Concepts

The Six Thinking Hats framework is often applied to generate new ideas or concepts. In this case, the session generally begins with green hat thinking followed by six-hat evaluation and upgrading of the best ideas.

Green Hat Thinking

Example #34

A business unit headquartered in Europe was holding an annual meeting with its 25 most important customers. The theme was "New Product Innovation," and an award was presented to the customer who had commercialized the most innovative new product. To reinforce the theme of their meeting, they were interested in an interactive three-hour creativity workshop to familiarize their customers with creativity tools and ways to apply them to practical business issues.

In the design meeting, an issue of common interest to the group was selected to demonstrate the value of a creative-thinking framework:

What processes might we use to find innovative applications for our products?

The participants were organized into teams and presented with the issue, and the Six Thinking Hats framework was overviewed as the framework that would be applied to creatively address the issue.

Yellow hat thinking was done first to warm up each team to the benefits of using a structured process to find innovative new applications for their products. Next, white hat thinking focused on information needed to design and implement such a process (e.g., consumer trends, technology forecasting, etc.). This was followed by black hat thinking to interact on barriers. Green hat thinking generated many ideas and concepts to overcome the barriers, and it provided insights into a possible process to find new applications for their products. This was aided by introducing them to lateral thinking that seeded many ideas beyond the first go-around of pattern thinking.

After harvesting the best ideas, the teams shared their output. Some participants were eager to return to their home base and implement ideas developed during the session as a way to accelerate development of new products.

Example #35

This example illustrates how the Six Thinking Hats framework can be applied to an important issue in education.

Six public school district superintendents in the state of Delaware and members of their staff met in a half-day session to deal with this issue:

How can we achieve third-grade reading capabilities for all students upon completion of third grade?

The group of 20 participants separated into three teams and selected the following three focus areas:

- *How can we focus on staff-development activities to promote and effect reading-instruction improvement?*
- *How can we increase the number of strategies available for reading instruction?*
- *How can we focus on early intervention strategies rather than remediation?*

Each team started with the green hat and generated numerous ideas using pattern thinking and then lateral thinking. Convergent thinking led each team to select the two best ideas, which were then evaluated and upgraded using six-hat thinking. Each team shared their thinking with the whole group, which then voted on the best idea to consider implementing. The selected idea:

Teach parents how to teach reading in the home.

The concept behind this idea was that most parents play a key role in teaching their children how to talk and how to walk and how to ride a bike . . . why not teach parents how to teach children how to read?

Planning for Implementation of an Idea

The following sequence of hats is a way to plan actions needed to implement best ideas harvested from a creative-thinking session:

Yellow Hat

- What factors favor the idea?
- Who would be supportive?

  Should we contact these people to gain early buy-in?

Black Hat

- What are the barriers?
- Who might oppose?

  Should we contact these people so we can understand their concerns?

Green Hat

- What are some ideas to overcome barriers?
- How might the original idea be upgraded?

Red Hat
- How might people react to the idea?
- Is the current environment favorable or unfavorable?
    Should we act now or wait? Should we poll reaction?

White Hat
- What information do we have?
- What information do we need?

Blue Hat
- Next steps/Responsibilities/Milestones?

Each hat stimulates thinking about what actions might be taken to implement the idea. The team then uses this as a basis for deciding on next steps.

Constructively Critiquing Meetings, Seminars, and Workshops

Many organizations sponsoring a meeting, seminar, or workshop want the audience to "rate" the event. The following sequence of hats focuses thinking on constructive suggestions to help improve future events:

White Hat
- What additional information in advance of or during the meeting would have been helpful?

Black Hat
- What was least beneficial in the meeting? What were the difficulties?

Yellow Hat
- What was most beneficial?

Green Hat
- What ideas for future meetings to increase value?

Red Hat
- How do I feel about this meeting?

Blue Hat
- How might the processes we used be improved?

Six Thinking Hats and Creativity Styles

The Six Thinking Hats framework generally works best with a mixed group of participants who range, in Michael Kirton's terms,[30] from highly "adaptive" to highly "innovative." The reason is that regardless of the hat the group is wearing, there is a more balanced input to the thinking process. Adaptive-style creative thinkers tend to express viewpoints consistent with existing structures, while innovative-style creative thinkers generate less conventional views.

In yellow hat thinking about a proposal, "adaptors" generally contribute important thoughts on the more obvious benefits, while "innovators" consider the proposal from different angles, contributing less obvious thoughts. In green hat thinking, "innovators" generate more unusual ideas and concepts while "adaptors" contribute ideas that are seen as more immediately acceptable. In blue hat thinking, "adaptors" are more comfortable and more likely to be the ones to summarize output of the session in an orderly way.

During the six-hat discussion, "adaptors" consistently follow the rules of parallel thinking, while "innovators" often stray and require reminders. Generally, adaptive-style thinkers and innovative-style thinkers contribute equally to the successful output of the Six Thinking Hats framework.

CREATIVE PROBLEM-SOLVING PROCESS

Many processes for creative problem solving are described in the literature.[2, 12, 24-25] In particular, pioneers at the State University College at Buffalo have published extensively. When the DuPont Center for Creativity & Innovation was formed, several problem-solving processes were benchmarked. Experienced facilitators selected for their workshops the elements from the benchmarked processes that they felt most comfortable with and best suited to meet the needs of the client.

This section overviews a creative problem-solving process that has been successfully applied in industry. It embodies some elements of published processes. A workshop generally takes one to three days. Basically, creative problem solving has three steps, each involving both divergent and convergent thinking:

Creative Problem-Solving Process

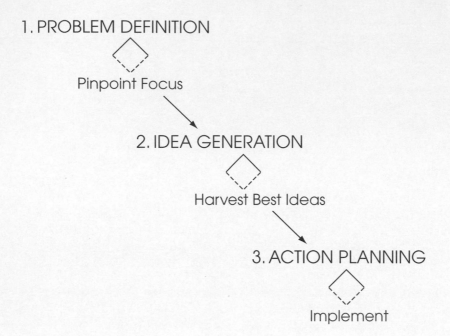

1. PROBLEM DEFINITION

Pinpoint Focus

2. IDEA GENERATION

Harvest Best Ideas

3. ACTION PLANNING

Implement

Problem Definition

The first step in the problem-solving process is to spend up-front time understanding and defining the client's problem (or opportunity). This is done in a design meeting held in advance of the workshop (described later in this section). It helps decide which participants to invite. The preferred number is generally 12–24, but can be as low as 4 and more than 30, depending on the situation.

FRANK AND ERNEST® by Bob Thaves

Problem statements can be on a general topic, such as: *How can we enhance our recruitment program?* or *How can we improve service of our central office staff to the business units?* Problem statements can be more specific, such as: *How can we reduce cash-flow cycle time from 200 to 50 days?* or *How can we reduce environmental waste in our plants by 80 percent?*

The first step in the workshop is for the client to describe to participants the broad problem statement and its background. The floor is then open for questions and answers so that everyone understands the problem being addressed.

Focus Areas

A vital step in the problem-solving process is to identify core issues within the broad problem statement on which to focus creative thinking. This step is sometimes the most challenging. It is the "peel the onion" step. The purpose is to get as close to the core of the issue as possible, where idea generation is most likely to pay off. The greater the specificity of the focus area, the better the chance of success in defining useful, implementable ideas.

To identify focus areas, the group uses divergent thinking that usually leads to 25–100 possible focus areas. Convergent thinking boils the list down to three to four that are perceived to be most important. The group is generally organized into teams, each choosing a focus area to carry through the idea-generation step. Techniques to develop possible focus areas are described below.

Wishful Thinking—This technique is popular with most facilitators. Participants are asked to think about a beneficial outcome related to the broad problem statement by completing the sentence:
   Wouldn't it be nice if (WIBNI)?

For example, on the problem of enhancing the recruitment program, a WIBNI might be: *Wouldn't it be nice if all potential recruits have personalized treatment during their visit?* The focus area would then be stated as: *How can we personalize the program for all recruits prior to and during their visit?*

Barriers to Overcome—This technique addresses barriers to achieving a solution to the broad problem statement. Participants are asked to complete this sentence:
   What stands in the way of . . . ?

For example, on the problem of reducing environmental waste in our plants, the question might be: *What stands in the way of the efficient tracking and measuring of waste?* Hence, the possible focus area would be: *How can we efficiently track and measure waste products in our plant?*

What's the "Real" Problem—This technique simply asks the group to list their thoughts on what they think is the problem underlying the broad problem. For example, if the problem statement is—*How can we spend less money on social welfare?*—some responses to the question of *What's the real problem?* might be *Too much money is spent on administration* or *Money isn't being spent properly* or *We don't have ways to measure properly* or *There's a low capability of people to get jobs* or *What's the criteria for being on welfare?* All of these can be converted into focus-area statements.

The "Why" Pursuit—This is a true "peel the onion" technique. The approach is to keep asking "Why" until a level of abstraction is specific enough to be a good focus area. For example, suppose the problem statement is:

  How can we increase yield in our fiber plant?

The discussion would follow this sequence:

- *Why is yield low? . . . Because of broken filaments.*
- *Why are there broken filaments? . . . Because of non-uniform polymer solution.*
- *Why is there non-uniform polymer solution?
    . . . Because the ingredients feed system is not working properly.*

Based on this sequence of *peel the onion*, the focus area selected would be:

  How can we get our ingredients feed system to work properly?

Trend Scenario—This technique is of value for many issues, such as: *How can we capture the owner-builder housing market?* The approach would be for the group to first list current trends in the market—*What is happening now?* Then the group would list their views on creative future possibilities. Based on the future scenario, they can now develop a host of future needs or opportunities that can form the basis for focus areas.

Metaphoric Thinking—Metaphoric thinking was used to develop focus areas in a problem-solving session on this issue: *How can I improve my sick business?* See Example #10, pp. 20–21.

Point of View—Sometimes, in developing focus areas, the group can be asked to look at this problem from different points of view. For example, in tackling this problem: *How can we capture the owner-builder housing market?* the group can be divided into teams, one to develop focus areas from the point of view of the homeowner, another of the builder, and another of the materials supplier. All focus areas are pooled, from which a balanced set can be selected for the idea-generation step.

Idea Generation

In this step, creative-thinking techniques are applied to generate ideas in each selected focus area. It is best to start with team members expressing ideas within normal thinking patterns. This has the benefit of collecting good ideas that people may have brought with them to the meeting, and it is a good warm-up.

To have everyone participate, it is best to alternate between individual thinking and group sharing. An effective process is to have each team member write his or her ideas on 3"x 5" Post-it® notes (one idea per note), read the ideas out loud to help trigger other people's thoughts, and hand the notes to the facilitator for posting on a hang chart.

After individuals have exhausted their ideas using normal thinking patterns and shared them with team members, the facilitator introduces creative-thinking tools. These are then applied to stimulate thinking outside normal thinking patterns. Facilitators have different preferences regarding tools they find most effective and feel comfortable teaching. Tools like lateral thinking always lead to a flow of many additional ideas that are often more unusual than previous ones.

Harvesting

A team of six people addressing a focus area will usually generate 50–150 ideas posted on hang charts. The challenge is to harvest the ones the team enthusiastically wants to implement. The selection process varies, but often is based on a set of criteria formulated by the team. The most frequently selected criteria: high business stakes; different from current thinking; doable.

After deciding on selection criteria, team members individually examine all the ideas that were posted and vote on the three they favor. Voting can be done by colored pencil check marks or colored Post-it® dots. This usually narrows the field to five to ten ideas, some of which have elements in common. Sometimes rewording is necessary to capture the essence of each idea. Generally, the team winds up with three to six ideas to consider for implementation. The harvesting process sometimes collects ideas in different categories, e.g., near-term/long-term or most practical/most unusual.

The Six Thinking Hats framework is often applied to evaluate and upgrade harvested ideas. This helps in the final selection of the idea(s) the team chooses for action planning.

Action Planning

One-third of the total creative problem-solving session should be devoted to action planning. This is an essential step. Otherwise, sessions are concluded with many excellent ideas, but good intentions are often lost when people return to urgent matters at their desks. Each organization likely has its own process for action planning. The format based on the Six Thinking Hats framework described in the previous section works well.

As a final step in a creative problem-solving session, a spokesperson for each team shares output in the following sequence: focus area selected; best ideas generated; actions proposed; and reflections on the process.

Design Meeting

Success of a problem-solving workshop will depend on the quality of advance planning. This is the reason for having a design meeting in advance of the workshop. The objective is to develop with the client a game plan that includes understanding the issue to be addressed, client expectations and goals, participants, and logistics such as length, location, and dates. The design meeting should be held several weeks in advance of the workshop to enable scheduling of invitees.

Participants—Selection of participants is a critical part of the design meeting. A problem-solving workshop generally has 12–24 participants divided into teams of 4–6. Those present should include the client, at least one decision maker, potential implementers of harvested ideas, and at least one "wild card."

A "wild card" is a person who is known to be an energetic creative thinker, but who is not close to the issue being addressed.

Participants who are knowledgeable about the issue and who have special expertise are essential. For example, a workshop addressing a groundwater contamination problem at a fiber manufacturing site was successful because in the design meeting it was decided to invite people having special expertise in the oil industry. They were knowledgeable about underground technology, which provided breakthrough ideas on how to cost-effectively remove groundwater contaminants.

Depending on the issue, it is preferable to have a multifunctional group of marketing, manufacturing, human resources, finance, technical, and business-based people. Attention should be paid to having people with diverse thinking styles. Sometimes it's of value to invite special guests such as a customer, supplier, secretary, plant operator, etc.

Often, participants have multiple roles. For example, in a design meeting where the workshop issue involved reducing plant environmental waste, it was suggested that the client invite a community leader who was interested in protecting the environment and who would also be a "wild card." The client invited a Catholic priest, who brought a fresh perspective to the issue, stimulated new insights in others, and contributed excellent ideas.

Facilitator Role

The role of the facilitator is to arrange a focused design meeting and lead the problem-solving process. Workshop success depends on quality of participant input and output, and on the skill of the facilitator to control group dynamics and process flow.

Good facilitators keep the process on track, improvise process changes as required, sense the best creativity tools to apply, let everyone have equal airtime, and assist in harvesting group output, usually on hang charts and/or transparencies.

Facilitator qualities, training, and certification standards are discussed in Chapter VII in the section describing the DuPont Center for Creativity & Innovation Facilitator Network.

Workshop Examples

Chapter VII has several examples of creative problem-solving workshops (Examples #47–52).

SYNECTICS

The Synectics system has been called by some an artificial vacation, because it seems to let us take a holiday from the problem by not having to think about it consciously for a while, and it encourages us to put aside our business-suit thinking, our usual tight, analytical frame of mind; but it is an artificial vacation, because while our conscious enjoys making the analogies, our preconscious is hard at work on the problem.

George M. Prince

Synectics is a problem-solving framework developed by W. J. J. Gordon and George M. Prince that uses metaphoric thinking as the main creative thinking tool.[12-13] Courses are available.[14] The Synectics framework has the following basic steps:

1. *The Problem (or Opportunity) as Given*—This is the problem statement to be attacked. Analysis in Synectics is explanation of the problem by the expert (owner of the problem).

2. *Goals as Understood*—This step identifies possible focus areas where the group uses the technique of wishful thinking. It helps break complex problems into manageable parts. The client selects the focus area to work on.

3. *Mental Excursion*—This step involves "taking a vacation from the problem" using several approaches to metaphoric thinking. For example, the leader challenges participants to think of examples of phenomena that are similar to the subject at hand. He or she then chooses an example that is interesting, strange, or irrelevant to the problem.

4. *Force Fit*—This is considered the most difficult step in the Synectics procedure. This is where the metaphorical material must be forced to be useful, even if it seems irrelevant to the problem. It is the point in the process for generating breakthrough ideas relevant to solving the problem. Prince uses the stories of Archemedes in the bathtub and Isaac

Newton beneath the apple tree to illustrate how an irrelevant stimulus can provoke a flash of inspiration.

5. *Viewpoint*—This is the step where possible solutions to the problem are selected for pursuing. Before an idea is accepted as a viewpoint, it must satisfy these two criteria:

- The expert (problem owner) must believe that the idea has new elements and is promising.

- The expert must know exactly what next steps to take to test its validity.

A session is considered successful if the expert has at least five viewpoints to act on.

Many practical examples illustrating the Synectics step-wise process are described in the book *Synectics*.[12] Synectics has been applied at DuPont to tackle various manufacturing problems, such as: *How can we increase uniformity of fiber finish application?* and *How can we reduce streaks produced from bulked continuous filament nylon?*

CONCEPT FAN

The concept fan is an Edward de Bono framework used to generate many alternatives for achieving a defined task.[9] Starting with the task and working backward, participants define broad directions (or focus areas), then concepts bearing on each direction, and finally actionable ideas related to the concept. This approach leads to a cascading of concepts and ideas to accomplish the task. The cascading of concepts and ideas is reversible. For example, sometimes participants find it easier to start the process with an idea, then define the concept involved in that idea, and then generate additional ideas related to the concept.

Example #36

In a 1990 meeting of the Edward de Bono International Creative Forum, the company representatives were dealing with this issue:

How can we meet the needs of our customers in the year 2000?

It was assumed that the customer then might be ten years old now. Hence, the task was defined as follows:

How can we access ten-year-olds?

The concept fan was as follows:

Concept Fan

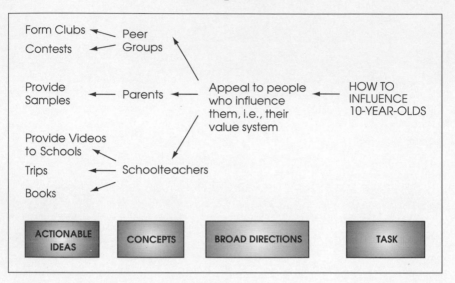

PROBLEM-SOLVING WALKAROUND

A new perspective about a problem might be gained by viewing it from the four different thinking modes of the Ned Herrmann whole-brain model:

- Upper Left Brain—An analytic, logical, rational "bottom line" view.

- Lower Left Brain—An organized, detailed, chronological view.

- Upper Right Brain—An intuitive, conceptual, visual, "big picture" view.

- Lower Right Brain—An interpersonal, emotional, "people" view.

The problem-solving walkaround framework was applied in a DuPont leadership meeting to think through this issue:

How can we educate DuPonters about the value of creativity and innovation?

The process is described in Example #38, p. 63.

PMI

The PMI is an Edward de Bono focused thinking model for treatment of ideas where:

- **"P"** stands for what's **Plus** about the idea, i.e., the good points.
- **"M"** stands for what's **Minus** about the idea, i.e., the bad points.
- **"I"** stands for what's **Interesting** about the idea, i.e., points that are neither good nor bad, but are worth noting.

The PMI is the first lesson of the Edward de Bono CoRT thinking lessons being widely used in schools for the direct teaching of thinking as a basic skill.[26] The PMI is a useful framework to get rapid feedback on an idea. It helps bypass people's natural emotional reaction to the idea.

Example #37

A motivational video was being prepared for a major conference to illustrate the value of day-to-day ideas in the innovation process. The video was in draft form and ready for critical review prior to finalizing. That week, there was a new employee orientation program with a one-hour session scheduled to introduce the field of creative thinking. This provided an opportunity to teach the PMI to the 30 participants and concurrently apply it to a practical issue, namely to critique the proposed video.

The PMI framework was explained, and the video was shown. Within about 20 minutes, the group learned the PMI and applied it to the video. This session provided constructive input that led to a much-improved video. For example, some of the minus points were that it was too long and that the narrator was too "professional," which gave the impression of a TV commercial. Some of the plus points were the basic message and the lively music. Some of the interesting points related to the general flow and visual effects.

OTHER CREATIVITY TECHNIQUES

Many other creative-thinking techniques exist that have not been covered here. An abundance of them can be found in Sydney J. Parnes' *Sourcebook for Creative Problem Solving*[25] and Edward Glassman's *Creativity Handbook.*[2] New techniques continue to be developed, such as Marilyn Schoeman Dow's Brain on Fast Forward (BOFF-O).[27]

The Second Dimension: Valuing Diversity in Thinking

While thinking skills are important in successful problem solving, another essential ingredient is diversity. This chapter describes frameworks dealing with diversity in thinking preferences and creativity styles. A person's behavior is also important since it doesn't always mirror preferred styles and preferences. Hence, another section discusses behavior patterns of creative thinkers and doers.

THINKING PREFERENCES

HERRMANN BRAIN DOMINANCE INSTRUMENT

The brain is specialized—not just physically, but mentally as well. Its specialized modes can be organized into four separate and distinct quadrants—each with its own language, perceptions, values, gifts, and ways of knowing and being. We are all unique composites of those differing modes according to our particular mix of mental preferences and avoidances.

Ned Herrmann

Ned Herrmann, an artist, a physicist by training, and a former Manager of Management Education at General Electric, is the father of the Brain Dominance Instrument.[28] The instrument integrates the scientific study of the brain with the study of creative human development. This section briefly overviews the Herrmann Brain Dominance Instrument (HBDI) and its practical applications. HBDI certification is available.[29]

HBDI Theory

The basic concept of the Herrmann model is that the brain is composed of four interactive quadrants, each representing a different category of preferences. Taken together, these four quadrants form a "whole brain," which profiles a person's thinking and behavior.

Whole Brain Model

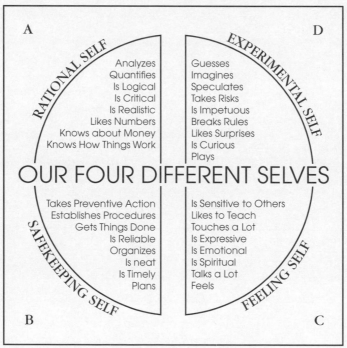

© 1997 The Ned Herrmann Group

For most people, the upper left quadrant (A), is better at performing analytical, logical, and mathematical activities and tasks. In contrast, the upper right quadrant (D), is better at imaginative, intuitive, and risky activities and tasks. In other words, the upper left brain does well at arithmetic and can solve problems through reason and logic. The upper right brain operates outside the norm, gets flashes of ideas, and solves problems on the basis of feelings and hunches.

The two lower quadrants are the focal points of the more visceral forms of mental processing. Structured, sequential, and organized mental activities are processed in the lower left quadrant of the brain (B). Emotional and interpersonal mental activities occur in the lower right quadrant (C). Taken together, the two cerebral hemispheres (A and D), and the two limbic hemispheres (B and C) form four different modes of thinking, which Ned Herrmann defines as our four different selves. For most of us, there is a brain dominance condition in which the quadrants work together, but with one or two taking the lead.

Measurement

The HBDI has 120 questions that measure thinking preferences on a scale of 1–100 to predict behavior.

Herrmann Brain Dominance Profile

© 1997 The Ned Herrmann Group

Over a million men and women's brain dominance profiles have been assessed by the HBDI. The strong correlation between HBDI and human behavior soundly validates the theory.

Representative Dominance Profiles

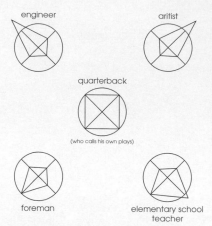

© 1997 The Ned Herrmann Group

Whole-Brain Thinking

Whole-brain thinking is particularly important in problem solving and dealing with difficult challenges. The HBDI profiles of members of a hospital staff is a good example. In hospitals, the doctors, nurses, administrators, and psychiatrists each have different primary preferences.

Herrmann Brain Dominance Profiles

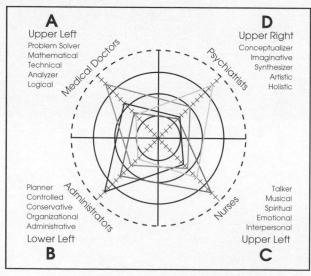

© 1997 The Ned Herrmann Group

Doctors score high in the A quadrant, nurses score high in C, administrators high in B, and psychiatrists high in D. Each of these groups generally form cliques in the hospital environment. However, in an emergency, since each of these preferences are essential, tribalism is suppressed, and all work together effectively as a whole-brain team.

Applications

There are many practical applications for the brain dominance concept, including problem solving, strategic business planning, and interpersonal relationships.

The Problem-Solving Walkaround

A new perspective about a problem might be gained by viewing it from the different modes of thinking. An individual or team might ask "How would my problem be viewed with sequential focus on each of the quadrants?" This "walking around" the problem might provide new insights toward a solution. The framework:

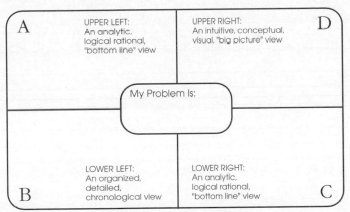

© 1997 The Ned Herrmann Group

Example #38

The following example illustrates how the problem-solving walkaround was applied to tackle a corporate issue.

In 1990, the DuPont company held a leadership meeting where one of the themes was the importance of diversity in achieving the corporate vision. The corporate Creativity and Innovation Committee organized a session with Ned Herrmann as the keynote speaker to stress the importance of diversity in thinking. Ned outlined brain dominance theory and provided feedback on the HBDI that all participants had taken prior to the meeting.

To illustrate the value of brain dominance theory in problem solving, a two-hour session for a portion of the audience was facilitated by Ted Coulson, Alison Strickland, and Ann Herrmann using the problem-solving walkaround. This framework was structured with a set of questions in each quadrant designed to stimulate whole-brain thinking on the central issue as shown below:

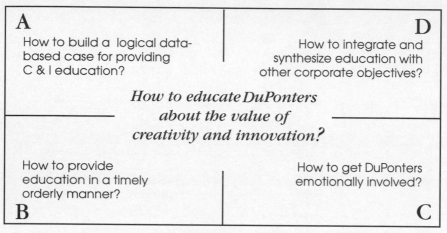

<table>
<tr><td>A
How to build a logical data-based case for providing C & I education?</td><td>D
How to integrate and synthesize education with other corporate objectives?</td></tr>
<tr><td colspan="2" align="center">How to educate DuPonters about the value of creativity and innovation?</td></tr>
<tr><td>How to provide education in a timely orderly manner?
B</td><td>How to get DuPonters emotionally involved?
C</td></tr>
</table>

© 1997 The Ned Herrmann Group

Ned Herrmann's seminar and this exercise supported the concept of establishing a DuPont Center for Creativity & Innovation (Chapter VII).

Example #39

This example illustrates how an HBDI provided new insights to a business director regarding his strategic-planning team.

A business director had his staff take the HBDI to gain insights about the diversity of thinking in the group. To his surprise, his core group of strategic planners, consisting of a marketing manager, a domestic strategist, an overseas strategist, and himself, had pronounced preferences, but supplementary differences in their brain dominances. One had strong preferences in the A and B quadrants, another in C and D, another in A and D, and another in B and C. Together, the four of them were a "perfect whole brain." From that time on, the director decided that he would not hold a strategic planning meeting unless all four of them were present.

Example #40

This example illustrates how an HBDI provided the author with new insights on the value of his secretary's diversity of thinking.

The author had attended the ACT-I workshop, explained the brain dominance theory to his secretary, Helen Snyder, and suggested that she take an HBDI. They compared results and were intrigued that between the two of them they comprised whole-brain thinking. He was prominent in the A and D quadrants, while she was prominent in B and C. From that time on, he consistently discussed key issues with his secretary to get another valuable point of view before making important decisions. She subsequently attended the ACT-I workshop, which further aided her understanding of creative thinking and motivated her to be a creativity champion.

FRANK AND ERNEST by Bob Thaves

HE JUST CAN'T WORK WITHOUT SUPERVISION --- I THINK IT'S TIME TO BRING ON EVE.

THAVES 8-19

Applied Creative-Thinking Workshop

A five-day workshop entitled "Applied Creative Thinking" (ACT-I), sponsored by the Ned Herrmann Group and facilitated by Ted Coulson and Alison Strickland, dramatically validates the brain dominance concept and application to problem solving.

About 20 applicants with diverse personalities are invited to attend the ACT-I workshop based on their HBDI scores. A group, for example, might include a self-employed entrepreneur, a corporate financial manager, an educator, a computer specialist, a journalist, a human resources manager, a technical manager, and a sculptor. Participants do not know the results of their HBDI until toward the end of the workshop.

Much of the workshop is devoted to problem solving in a variety of situations and in mixed groups. Problems involving logic caused some people great difficulty. However, when exposed to problems involving unfamiliar sounds, design of a personal logo, or expressing the problem using a three-dimensional metaphor, these same people were amazingly creative. The ones who found the logic-based problems simplistic were usually at a loss when it came to problems or exercises requiring imagination. Few people were good at both.

Working on a project or problem with someone who had a brain dominance profile similar or different from yourself gave quite different results. Working on a problem-solving team that had each brain dominance represented invariably led to a more balanced whole-brain solution.

The ACT-I workshop has a segment devoted to "dreaming a solution to a problem" that participants are asked to bring with them to the workshop. An example of how this exercise influenced the author's direction in thinking is described in Example #15, p. 24.

ACT-I Alumni Group

Several employees who had attended the ACT-I workshop formed an alumni group at the DuPont site in Richmond, Virginia. Led by Jean Prideaux, Technical Group Manager, this group of diverse individuals included engineers, scientists, secretaries, manufacturing people, and technicians. The objective was to apply creative-thinking techniques to practical problems presented by fellow employees. The story of how this group generated a creative idea that put back on track a program with a $30 million stake is discussed in Example #44, p. 80. This example of success was described by the key players in a videotape shown at the leadership conference described in Example #38, p. 63.

CREATIVITY STYLES

FRANK AND ERNEST © by Bob Thaves

THE KIRTON ADAPTION-INNOVATION INVENTORY

Michael Kirton, the renowned British psychologist, related over dinner a delightful story of how, at the age of seven, he observed that two relatives consistently behaved differently when confronted with identical situations. This astute observation ultimately led to the widely applied Kirton Adaption-Innovation Inventory (KAI) that measures people's creativity and problem-solving styles.[30] This section overviews the KAI and practical applications. KAI certification courses are available.[31]

Innovation in this section differs in meaning from other sections in this book where it is defined as "taking ideas to market."

Basic Assumptions

Michael Kirton's basic assumptions in the Adaption-Innovation Theory is as follows:

- All people are creative; everyone generates ideas (novelty); everyone problem solves.

- As far as brain operation is concerned, creativity and problem solving seem indistinguishable. The distinction may be little more than linguistic.

- Everyone is a change agent. This fits well into Quality Management, where all are involved in quality operations.

- Adaption-Innovation theory distinguishes sharply between style and level. They do not correlate. Everyone can be measured on: How do I create? or How creative am I?

- Level is related to skill, IQ, and competency, much of which can be improved by learning.

- Style is unchanging throughout life. We can operate outside our preferred style by using coping behavior.

Excluding Kirton's own work, scholars have written 200 journal articles and 75 theses on his ideas since 1978. This research comes from several countries, notably the U.S. He attempts to dispose of the notion that *new* or *creative* is synonymous with *innovation*. Working within or across the paradigm are both worthy strategies, and their value is determined only by whether the problem gets solved. He comments that "a title like *Creativity and Innovation* is a sure way to confuse matters from the start."

Styles

The Adaption-Innovation Theory postulates that people are creative and solve problems, to a greater or lesser degree, on a continuum of styles from *adaptive* to *innovative*.

> *The more adaptive:* Prefer to make existing systems better; solve problems within existing paradigms; prefer a structured approach; are precise and dependable; and bring order and stability into novelty.

> *The more innovative:* Prefer to make existing systems different; solve problems with less regard to existing paradigms; prefer an unstructured approach; may be unique and visionary; and bring solutions that are hard to sell.

A successful organization has a range of adaptors and innovators. Both can generate novelty. The former does it within the system, the latter with less regard to current practice, policy, systems, and paradigms. Everyone, wherever they fall on the Adaption-Innovation range, is liable to produce a new product. The adaptor's product is likely to be an improvement on an existing general model—doing the job better. The innovator's product is more likely to be radical—doing it differently. However, they all need one another. For instance, a highly innovative product will undoubtedly need further development, especially from adaptors, who will strive to make it more practical and more cost-effective. Most people are not at the extreme of either direction in the continuum, but have a preference in one direction or the other.

Adaptors often view innovators as unsound, impractical, and a source of confusion, even if they are stimulating and challenging.

Innovators view adaptors as conforming, timid, and stuck in a "rut," even if they are dependable, sound, and expert on detail.

FRANK & ERNEST® by Bob Thaves

A person's creative-thinking style is stable and related to personality. However, behavior is flexible. The ability to shift style under circumstances where shifts are desirable is termed *coping*. Some people are better able to cope than others. Understanding the Adaption-Innovation Theory generally helps people become more conscious of the need to cope, particularly relative to other styles in a team situation. They realize that the primary focus is to solve the problem with the help of others on the continuum rather than despite them.

Measurement

The KAI, as a measure of the theory, is an instrument that yields a score that distinguishes adaptors and innovators on a continuum. KAI is normally distributed in all populations known, including the U.S., Britain, France, Canada, the Netherlands, and Italy.

Styles of Creativity

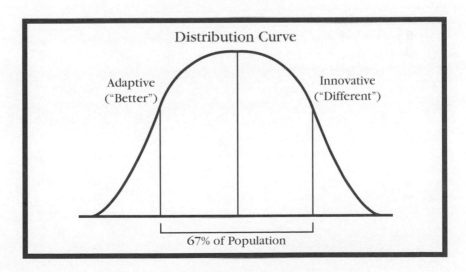

In filling out the KAI Inventory, there are no right or wrong answers. Preference for a more adaptive or a more innovative approach to problem solving is not good or bad. Each has its own contribution in dealing with a given issue. To obtain valid results, it is particularly important that answers represent how the person views himself or herself actually to be . . . not as he or she wants to be (or wants others to perceive him or her to be).

A purpose of the KAI is to help individuals understand their own and other people's preferences and behavior patterns. This aids relationships and performance. Effective range of KAI is just over 100 points. People who know each other well can accurately detect a ten-point difference in their scores: "He/she is a little more adaptive (or innovative) than I." A difference of 20 points can lead to conflict and discomfort. Larger differences can lead to serious communication problems. Understanding others' differences leads to admiration and respect. Those who have an intermediate KAI score to other individuals or groups have potential to act as "bridges," as long as they are willing and have the skills.

Relationship of KAI and the Six Thinking Hats Framework

The Edward de Bono Six Thinking Hats framework, discussed in Chapter IV, generally works best with a mixed group of participants who range, in KAI terms, from highly adaptive to highly innovative.

Regardless of the hat the group is wearing, a mixed group of adaptors and innovators provide a more balanced input to the thinking process. For example, in yellow hat thinking on a proposal, adaptors generally contribute important thoughts on the more obvious benefits, while innovators consider the proposal from different angles, contributing thoughts on less obvious benefits. In green hat thinking, innovators generate more unusual ideas and concepts, while adaptors contribute ideas that are seen as more immediately acceptable. In blue hat thinking, adaptors are more comfortable and more likely to be the ones to summarize output of the session in an orderly way.

During the six-hat discussion, the adaptors consistently follow the rules of parallel thinking, while the innovators often stray and require reminders. Generally, adaptors and innovators contribute equally to the successful output of the Six Thinking Hats framework.

Applications

There are many practical applications for KAI, including strategic resourcing of task forces, structuring committees, personnel hiring, problem solving, enhancing customer relationships, leading meetings, and being an effective educator.

Example #41

The following example illustrates how the KAI provided guidance in resourcing a task force.

A senior executive had heard about KAI in a creative-thinking seminar. He was in the process of resourcing a task force to implement an important facet of a strategic plan. He requested that a KAI be run on his total organization to provide insights on selection of task force members.

The KAI showed that his organization was biased in the direction of adaptor, which he felt was generally appropriate for his business and consistent with his style. However, there were a few individuals whose styles, relative to the rest, were innovative. Recognizing the value of diversity in thinking styles, this helped guide him in selection of task force members, some of whom had been identified as more innovative by the KAI.

Example #42

This example illustrates how a KAI in advance of forming an advisory committee would have likely created a more balanced and productive committee.

A Corporate Advisory Committee was formed to help guide a creativity effort. Members were selected who were known to be highly creative thinkers and strong supporters of this creativity effort. After a period of operation, committee members agreed to a KAI as a learning experience. The KAI showed that, with the exception of one member, all had styles biased in the direction of strongly innovative. In hindsight, the organizers of the committee realized that more attention should have been paid in selecting a more diverse group of thinkers, which would have likely led to a more productive committee.

Example #43

This example illustrates the importance of paying attention to KAI theory in hiring CEOs.

The CEO of a global company was holding his annual meeting of 60 senior executives from sites located in different parts of the world. The three-day meeting included a one-day seminar on creative-thinking techniques, styles, and applications. The part of the seminar dealing with diversity in thinking styles included feedback on a KAI that was run prior to the meeting. While not disclosed at the seminar, it was interesting that the relatively new CEO scored highly innovative, while the rest of the organization was biased toward adaption. The owner of the company, a banker, demonstrated during the conversation at lunch that he was clearly adaptive.

About a year after the meeting, the CEO left the company. This was predictable, since his management style clearly did not fit the culture of this conservative company. If this was the case, then both the owner and CEO would have benefited from a more thorough consideration of importance of thinking styles, either in the original selection or on how to use the diversity effectively.

Other Examples

There are numerous situations where practical application of KAI is of value. In organizing a creative problem-solving workshop, facilitators often run a KAI on participants in advance of the event to help form teams with a good balance of thinking styles. Balance is itself subject to team review, as the "best" balance for a team is the one that solves the current problem. The next problem may call for a different balance.

Salespersons familiar with KAI often plan a sales pitch based on their perception of the customer's thinking style. A salesperson having an extreme innovator style would have trouble making the sale to a customer having adaptor bias, unless he or she were able to "cope" with the situation and organize his or her pitch accordingly.

Leaders familiar with KAI are conscious of the diversity of thinking styles in their staff group and act as a "bridge," particularly in dealing with controversial issues.

Educators familiar with KAI are conscious of the importance of organizing their lessons in a way that appeals to both the more adaptive and more innovative students.

BEHAVIOR PATTERNS

While people's thinking preferences and creativity styles differ, there are certain behavior patterns that creative thinkers and doers have in common. The following six behavior patterns are characteristic of creative thinkers and doers:

- *They have an absolute discontent with the status quo.*
  Hence, they constantly search for ways to constructively improve current practices. These people are sometimes viewed as "troublemakers," but they often come up with the most creative ideas and drive them to reality. People don't have to be troublemakers to be creative thinkers and movers.

- *They seek alternative solutions to problems or opportunities.* They don't grab at the first idea, but they take time to search for alternatives, sometimes applying creativity tools like lateral thinking and metaphoric thinking, which help stir the imagination.

- *They have a "prepared" mind.* Creative thinkers are alert to things around them that may trigger ideas to meet important needs. Many discoveries often attributed to circumstances or luck occur because the inventor had a "prepared" mind. Example #24 on p. 30 describes how having a prepared mind played a part in the invention of spunbonded sheet structures.

- *They think positively.* Sometimes negative results are a blessing in disguise. Creative thinkers turn a negative into a positive by viewing it from different angles. Example #20 on pp. 27–28 describes the role of positive thinking in the discovery of dye-resistant nylon, a key product in DuPont's carpet line. In the cartoon on p. 74, looking at a curved flashlight beam as a problem with worn batteries could be viewed instead as the discovery of a flashlight that shines around corners.

- *They know when they have a good idea and "champion" it.* They don't give up, but aggressively seek options to sell their idea. A good example is described in Chapter IX, where the idea of a crawfish bait was initially rejected by the business unit as not being pertinent to their business. The champions created suction for the product by giving samples to fishermen, which created a demand for the product.

- *They work hard at it.* A study at the University of California of known creative thinkers (famous writers, artists, composers, and inventors) showed that of the many characteristics that emerged, only one was common to them all—an intense interest in working hard at what they were doing. This is exemplified by the manufacturing person described in Example #14, p. 23, who lay in his bed with the plant problem "throbbing in his head like a toothache." He dreamed of a possible solution, and he went to work before sunrise to try it.

The above behavior characteristics are not necessarily innate. To be a creative thinker and doer, it helps for a person to take the time to question the status quo, seek alternative solutions to problems by sometimes applying creativity tools, have a "prepared" mind, think positively, champion his or her ideas, and work hard at it.

The Third Dimension: Engaging the Organization

It is insufficient for an organization to have creative, innovative individuals. The environment must be structured for creative tension, positive turbulence around a vision, and the space and freedom for people to "dance with their ideas" without fear of mistakes.

Paraphrased from talks given at a 1986 Creativity Week Symposium held at the Center for Creative Leadership, Greensboro, North Carolina

FRANK AND ERNEST® by Bob Thaves

DIVISIONAL PILOT

This chapter describes the approach taken by the author, as Divisional R & D Technical Director, to introduce creative-thinking techniques into the DuPont Industrial Fibers Division. In hindsight, this effort served as a pilot program, whose learnings were applied in organizing and operating the DuPont Center for Creativity & Innovation.

In the mid-1980s, the Industrial Fibers Technical Division's seven businesses were operating in an environment of fierce, competitive pressure. Quality and continuous-improvement programs were underway, similar to competitors. This was essential but not enough! Maintaining leadership required a bolder approach that placed higher priority on the generation of new ideas and concepts. To accomplish this, it was necessary to provide a more supportive environment for creative thinking and innovation.

SUPPORTIVE ENVIRONMENT

The challenge to provide a more creative, innovative environment is as difficult as any culture change, requiring ongoing support and patience. Human nature is to resist change, resist "another program," and regard the effort as just another "whim" of current management. The approach taken was to avoid referring to this effort as a "program" and to "just do it." A culture-change model provided an excellent framework to accomplish the task.

CULTURE-CHANGE MODEL

Many components contribute to culture change. One way to categorize these is through a culture-change model designed by Charlie Krone, a DuPont consultant. Facilitator Harold Stroupe applied the Krone model at a quality leadership meeting. It triggered the idea of how to approach the task of enhancing the environment for creativity and innovation.

A culture can be defined by four components and changed by shifting these components. The anthropological terms are: 1. Status (standards); 2. Rituals (repetitive interactions); 3. Totems (emblems of success); 4. Taboos (deterrents). The following was a model applied in the Industrial Fibers Division to enhance the environment for creativity and innovation:

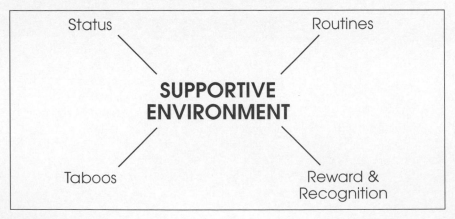

Status

This is where we are grounded—the base point. Status directly reflects values, i.e., the relative importance we give to things or people in an endeavor. All other components must be coordinated and in concert with status. The routines, reward and recognition, and taboos are a function of status. There is often overlap between these components.

The divisional effort was aided by a corporate initiative in the fall of 1985 that gave status to the need for renewed innovation. A company-wide innovation audit was conducted by Gifford Pinchot and Company to determine supports and barriers to bringing new ideas to market. The value for creativity and innovation was further reinforced by DuPont Chairman Ed Woolard, who was quoted in a DuPont magazine interview as saying:

> *We intend to provide hero status to those who show us how to get products to the marketplace more creatively.*

The first step in the divisional effort was to publicize corporate actions to provide a sound base-point on value. This was done in local seminars given by the Technical Director to R & D groups located at six plant sites.

Concurrently, the Technical Director began attending external creativity and innovation seminars and workshops to become educated in the field. This helped identify those who would be of most value to the organization. Learnings from these seminars and workshops were publicized by issuing highlights to all technical unit heads and group managers. This gave divisional status to the effort and communicated knowledge about creativity tools, processes, and frameworks. A general reaction from the professionals was, "So that's what creativity is about."

Further status to the effort was added by scheduling quality time for employees to learn and apply creativity tools. This was done by the Technical Director occasionally substituting monthly site-visitation technical program reviews with a day-long creativity seminar and workshop. Hence, while something new was added, something else was deleted. Early seminar speakers included Edward de Bono on lateral thinking, Ned Herrmann on whole-brain thinking, and Roger von Oech on creative blockbusting. The morning was devoted to learning the creativity tools and the afternoon to cross-functional teams applying the learnings to practical problems.

The on-site seminars and workshops exposed employees to creativity gurus firsthand and enabled them to experience the value of creativity as a skill. Employees became motivated to learn more. They began reading books and requesting attendance at external seminars and workshops. Site libraries began stocking pertinent books and publications. Hundreds of technical people were issued *de Bono's Thinking Course*.[8] The education process was underway. Champions sprouted and began applying their learnings to job-related problems, both individually and in teams. Successes were publicized—many examples are described throughout this book.

Awareness of creativity tools and interest in their value spread from the R & D units to manufacturing, marketing, and business-planning functions. Business managers and functional directors attended meetings to discuss ways to apply creativity tools across the division. This led to formulation of a vision:

- Creativity and innovation are valued at all levels in the organization, and management behavior consistently signals and reinforces this value.

- Employees are knowledgeable about the technology of creativity and innovation and are applying the skills they develop.

- Employees have the space and take the time to be more creative and innovative.

Multifunctional committees were formed to implement the vision.

Further status was gained by the appointment of a divisional Creativity Manager, Alex de Dominicis. He became thoroughly versed in creative-thinking techniques by attending many seminars and workshops. For example, he attended a one-week lateral thinking training course in Europe conducted by Edward de Bono. The Divisional Organization Effectiveness Facilitator, Dick Comer, added creative-thinking tools to his kit of expertise. For example, he became certified in Ned Herrmann's Brain Dominance Instrument (Chapter V). Both began receiving many requests from business and functional units to facilitate creative-thinking workshops.

Routines

Many repetitive interactions were initiated to help foster a creative environment and cascade awareness of the value of creative thinking throughout the division from 1986 to 1990.

These were rooted through actions initiated by both upper management and site creativity champions.

Creativity Social Hours

An effective way to cascade creativity awareness was to hold Creativity Social Hours during the Technical Director's monthly management visits to R & D units. These coffee-and-cake sessions were held at the end of the day following program reviews. In advance of the visit, the unit head was asked to identify two or three individuals in his organization who had thought of a creative idea in their program and were implementing it. These people were presented a Creative Thinking Award that consisted of a dinner for two and a miniature statue of Rodin's *The Thinker*.

The request to the unit head stimulated him to think about who in his organization was doing creative work that merited recognition. What is the first thing he would ask his group managers in his weekly staff meeting? *Who in your group has been doing creative work lately?* This had the effect of cascading through the management line an increased awareness and interest in creative work being done in the unit.

Another benefit of the Creativity Social Hour was to educate employees about creative thinking by highlighting examples of success. This was done by the award recipients themselves who agreed to describe their "Aha" and how they were applying it in their program. It didn't matter whether the idea originated using a creativity tool or by normal patterns of thinking. The highlight of the meeting was the enthusiasm of the recipients as they described their creative contributions.

Asking people to be creative is like asking a child to be good. They don't know what you mean. Hearing colleagues describe how creativity helped them in their work gave meaning to creativity. Engineers in the plant process units originally felt that creativity was only for research people. This changed when they heard a fellow engineer describe how a creative idea helped him increase productivity of a manufacturing process by 20 percent versus the goal of only 5 percent. Now they understood what was meant by *creative thinking* and how it might benefit them. Hence, they became more involved in the unit's creativity effort.

People love to discuss their creative work. In the several years of Creativity Social Hours, every award recipient, even the most introverted, enthusiastically agreed to describe his or her work, always crediting team members for their contributions. The metaphoric thinking success described in Example #9, p. 20, that solved the dyeable Nomex® problem, was first aired by the inventor at one of these Creativity Social Hours.

Monthly Meetings of ACT-I Alumni Group

An ACT-I Alumni Group was formed with members that had attended the Ned Herrmann Applied Creative Thinking workshop (Chapter V). The meetings were initiated and championed by Jean Prideaux, Kevlar® Technical Group Manager, at the Richmond, Virginia, plant. The purpose was to apply creative-thinking techniques to difficult problems brought to the meeting by fellow employees.

Example #44

This example illustrates the kinds of problems that were tackled by the ACT-I alumni group.

A team of technical engineers had run into a dead-end in scaling up a new process that had been demonstrated in the laboratory. The stake in succeeding with this new process was $30 million. As a last resort, they met with the ACT-I alumni group. The creative-thinking session generated many ideas using a variety of creativity techniques. The result was an elegant idea worth testing. It worked, and the development proceeded.

Peer-Group Innovation Award

The Kevlar® technical unit sponsored a monthly innovation award, championed by Syd Gauntt, Engineering Associate. Recipients were nominated by their peers and received an inscribed plaque. This local event was another routine that site champions put in place to support the environment for creativity and innovation.

Green Hat Creativity Group

A Green Hat Creativity Group, initiated and championed by Ray Hannah, Technical Group Manager at the Chattanooga nylon plant, met monthly. Their approach was to attack difficult technical and manufacturing problems presented by colleagues using the Edward de Bono Six Thinking Hats framework, which he had taught in a plant seminar. They would start out with green hat generation of ideas to solve the problem using lateral thinking and then evaluate best ideas using the six-hat framework. In this way, they not only applied these techniques in group problem solving, but also gained experience for future use. An example was to apply the framework to create new concepts for collecting and stabilizing a new fiber under development.

Creative Discoveries Workshop

This workshop, supported by Jean Prideaux and cochampioned by Jim Casto and Karen Gammon, technical employees at the DuPont Richmond plant, was designed to serve as an introductory creativity and innovation experience for Technical Assistants and other plant employees such as members of the Site Safety Network. It is based on a four-step creative problem-solving process that includes a component stressing the value of diversity within a team.

Quarterly Divisional Group Manager Meetings

Each quarter, the Technical Group Managers and Unit Heads met to discuss functional issues. Creativity became a routine agenda item. Early in the creativity effort, an entire quarterly meeting was devoted to the culture-change model. After learning the model, the group of about 40 participants divided into subgroups to discuss the four components of the model in terms of current practices, future possibilities, and recommended actions. This led to buy-in of the model and ownership of ideas. Some managers organized similar meetings with their groups.

Innovation News Items

Each technical unit routinely issued biweekly "What's New" reports. A new segment was added to this report entitled "Innovation News Items." This provided a platform for technical people to report on creativity and innovation items they felt would be of interest to readers. The contribution of the manufacturing employee who dreamed a solution to the collapsing hose problem described in Example #14, p. 23, was learned through this mechanism. Both the manufacturing person and the technical employee who took the trouble to report the creative contribution received a Creative Thinking Award.

Example #45

This example illustrates the type of innovation news items that were encouraged.

In a site creativity seminar, Roger von Oech suggested that employees challenge rules and assumptions that stand in the way of getting things done and seek creative ways around them. An employee was rewarded for the "Innovation News Item" shown below that exemplified this practice.

Sale of R & D Product (G. L. Hendrin)—A customer had requested a new product that is produced off-site. Due to computer program constraints, we were unable to use the normal plant shipping procedures and still meet the timing that the customer required. Personnel in our local accounting department provided guidance on selling the material as an R & D product, which allowed us to bypass the plant systems for this first order. In addition to meeting the customer's needs, the Nomex® Technical budget received a 40 percent profit on this order. The concept of turning Technical into a moneymaking venture of its own has been disposed of, and procedures were implemented to allow use of plant systems on future orders.

Creativity/Innovation Newsletter

A Creativity/Innovation newsletter was issued biweekly by Alex de Dominicis, the Divisional Creativity Manager who helped expand knowledge in the field. Alex drew on the literature and other sources for his newsletter. The newsletter was issued by electronic mail to all members of the division and the OZ Creative Thinking Network. An example is shown below.

CREATIVITY/INNOVATION NEWSLETTER

THE "GOLDEN EGG" AWARD

When a small group of presidents of Ann Arbor businesses decided to get together once a month for a variety of reasons, they soon found that a favorite part of their meeting was the sharing of mistakes and other misadventures.

The enthusiasm members felt for these sharings led to the idea of a "Golden Egg" award. As one member put it, "I want to hear it from the member who got egg on his face trying out his idea." A trophy was soon put together (with the help of a L'eggs® pantyhose container and some gold spray paint).

Presentation of this award for the best mistake of the month became a standard part of their meeting, and the trophy itself added an important new dimension. The winning president was expected to take the trophy back to his office and leave it on his desk for the entire month. The presence of the "Golden Egg" raised questions from visitors and led to telling the questioner how he got the award. It also gave the president a chance to be a model for treating mistakes as opportunities to learn how to do it better rather than as situations requiring blame. It legitimized the importance of learning from our failures and successes. Thus, the inscription of "Golden Egg Award Sharing Turns a Goose Egg Experience into a Golden Egg Idea."

A "Golden Egg" sharing session can be made a regular part of your meeting. In a supportive and encouraging atmosphere, the experiences shared are not only useful, but are frequently entertaining. But the ultimate value of the award lies in learning from mistakes rather than using them to punish, and the increase with time in trust, openness and creativity.

As with many of the suggestions written about in the C/I newsletter, they are as applicable in family situations as they are at work. That's right, kids, Mom and Dad are not perfect! What can we learn from their mistakes?

Special Events

The Richmond site held an annual December creativity seminar/buffet to which all site technical and support employees were invited. The most successful of these had as the speaker Dr. Annette Goodheart, a psychotherapist, who described the connection between laughter and creativity. Her message was: "Take your job seriously but yourself lightly." She told humorous stories about her huggable teddy bear. Miniature teddy bears were given to the 200 attendees. The following day, teddy bears showed up on many desks in the workplace as a reminder of the message.

Reward and Recognition

Rewards are often pay-off centered versus investment-centered . . . unwillingness to bet on potential means that much potential innovation is lost.

Rosabeth Moss Kanter, author of *Changemasters*

The divisional reward-and-recognition process did not wait until the point of financial pay-off, which did not always occur. Rewards were generally given when a creative idea was in the implementation stage. The main purpose was to reinforce the value of creative thinking by visibly recognizing role models.

The division established three awards: (1) the Creative Technology Award for breakthrough new technology of value to the business; (2) the Creative Thinking Award for day-to-day ideas that helped problem solving; and (3) the Creative Leadership Award for group managers who played an active role in championing creativity and innovation. The awards were an inscribed statue of Rodin's *The Thinker* and a monetary gift.

Awards were presented to individuals and teams in the presence of their peers at the Creativity Social Hours or Quarterly Technical Manager meetings described above. This provided a platform to raise awareness on the value placed by management on creative thinking and behavior. Line managers were responsible to recommend award recipients. Therefore, they became more alert to creative behavior of their people, which in turn further reinforced status.

Reward and recognition of the type described above did not take the place of merit raises and promotion or other mechanisms in the company for outstanding performance.

Taboos

These are behaviors that are contrary to the values we seek to affirm, i.e., things that need to be eliminated from the culture.

An example of a taboo is to react negatively when a colleague suggests an idea, even though it may appear to have no value. The idea should be considered as a possible stepping stone to other ideas that may have great value.

Another taboo is to punish employees for taking a risk that didn't pan out. Emphasis should be on support of risk taking and focusing on learning from mistakes as described in the Creativity/Innovation Newsletter shown previously. An excellent article by Charles W. Prather on risk taking describes how the amount of innovation in an organization could depend on the way in which a mistake or failure is handled.[32]

MEASUREMENT

It has been said that "What gets measured gets done." What gets measured is also a message to the organization of what the management values.

CREATIVITY & INNOVATION QUESTIONNAIRE

A questionnaire on the climate for creativity and innovation is a measurement tool and also an effective vehicle to help create a supportive environment. It is the beginning of a dialogue between the people in the organization and the management.

Several good instruments exist to measure the climate:

- The Pinchot Innovation Audit—This audit identifies, through a questionnaire and interviews, supports and obstacles to innovation and then plots them on a map.[33] For example, the "obstacles map" has on one axis the level of difficulty to overcome, and on the other axis, the level of importance. This provides guidance on which obstacles are most important to overcome and the degree of anticipated difficulty.

- Situational Questionnaire—This questionnaire is based on the work of Goran Ekvall in Sweden and is refined and validated by Scott Isaksen and coworkers at the Center for Studies in Creativity, the State University College at Buffalo, and the Creative Problem-Solving Group—Buffalo, New York. This is a multimethod (quantitative and qualitative) tool in evaluating organizational climate.[34]

- The Creative Practices Survey—This survey was developed by Caleb S. Atwood and Rolf C. Smith. It polls factors that enhance or discourage creativity.[35]

- KEYS: The Work Environment Inventory—This inventory was developed by Professor Teresa Amabile and the Center for Creative Leadership and administered by Stan Gryskiewicz and Bob Burnside.

It focuses on factors in the work environment most likely to influence expression and development of creative ideas.[36] This inventory was used to measure progress in the Industrial Fibers Technical Division, as described in the following example:

Example #46

In April of 1988, 246 employees of the Industrial Fibers Technical Division located at five sites completed the Center for Creative Leadership Work Environment Inventory (short form). This was about 18 months after the start of the creativity and innovation effort. The inventory was administered by Robert M. Burnside of the Center for Creative Leadership. The purpose was to calibrate the climate in the division against a control group of 1,500 people from other organizations who had taken this inventory. In hindsight, it would have been beneficial to have also inventoried at the beginning of the effort.

Format

The inventory had 29 questions related to environmental creativity stimulants and 14 questions related to obstacles. The stimulant questions measured employee views on a scale of 1 to 5 toward freedom; sufficient resources; encouragement; challenge; reward & recognition; sufficient time; unity of cooperation; creativity supports; overall environment; coworkers; and supervisor. The obstacle questions measured views toward constraint; evaluation pressure; status quo; political problems; and structures.

Importantly, the study was conducted confidentially. The only published results were of the total division. Each unit head received results of his total unit, but not of the individual groups in his unit. Each group manager received results of his or her total group, but not of individuals in the group.

Results

Robert Burnside summarized results of the Work Environment Inventory at a Quarterly Technical Management meeting. Quotes from his memo dated May 8, 1988:

Overall environment for creativity compares favorably with CCL's norm group. The Industrial Fibers Technical Division consistently has a higher prevalence of stimulants and a lower presence of obstacles, and its employees give it a higher overall rating than our norm group employees. (Our norm group is composed of 1,500 employees in about 200 organizations).

Remarkable in the stimulants categories are the high rating (3.0) on encouragement and unity and cooperation. These are consistently low in the other organizations that we studied. In my research findings to date, I have highlighted encouragement as the stimulant category most needing skill development for managers. Their ratings differentiate it from most other organizations.

The results were gratifying, indicating that the effort was on the right track. However, some categories scored lower than others and needed attention. The most prevalent in the stimulant category was reward and recognition and in the obstacles category, inappropriate evaluation. These were related. It was later learned that the concerns centered on the trend at that time (1988) toward teams. Some people felt that as part of a team, their individual contributions were not recognized. This learning sensitized the managers to this issue, and they took steps accordingly.

IMPACT OF CREATIVE ENVIRONMENT ON INVENTIVENESS

An environment for creative thinking inspires inventiveness. It was no coincidence that during the period that the environment for creative thinking was enhanced in the DuPont Industrial Fibers Technical Division, the number of filed patent cases soared. In the three years following initiation of the effort, the annual notices of invention submitted by the R & D people surged from 40 in 1987 to 148 in 1989. In the same period, annual patent filings climbed from 16 to 67, foreign filings escalated from 99 to 383, and patent allowances almost tripled from 10 to 28. This increase in patent activity was also stimulated by a concurrent effort to increase awareness of the patenting process, but that is another story.

LEARNINGS

In reflection, these are learnings from the divisional creativity and innovation effort during the four- to five-year period beginning in 1986:

- Don't structure as a "Program"! People resent new programs.

- Start "doing" the following:

  - Educate self and others in creative-thinking skills.

  - Tie in with divisional and corporate principles.

  - Reinforce value continually (creativity events, reward and recognition).

  - Publicize role models and examples of success.

  - Support and protect champions.

  - Encourage risk taking by learning from, not punishing, mistakes.

- Top-down and grassroots support are both essential.

- Early successes are vital to help sustain momentum.

- Behavior change takes two to four years, but bottom-line payoff can begin soon.

An interesting observation in the divisional effort was that even units that were less participatory in learning and applying the new creative-thinking tools began to think and act more creatively. It wasn't important whether they used a new tool or not. They were encouraged that the management was supportive of creative thinking, provided space and freedom, encouraged risk taking, and did not punish mistakes but encouraged learnings.

The Fourth Dimension: Structuring for Creativity and Innovation

Unless you tend to the structures and systems, changes won't last. People slip back into old patterns, because ownership for change usually rests with the boss. They see their improvement effort as an extra task.

James Balasco, *Teaching the Elephant to Dance*

Several structures and systems were discussed in the previous chapter dealing with the introduction of creative-thinking techniques into an organization. This chapter describes structure and operation of the DuPont Center for Creativity & Innovation, the DuPont OZ Creative Thinking Network and the Fletcher Challenge Building Products Sector creativity program.

DUPONT CENTER FOR CREATIVITY & INNOVATION

In 1989, DuPont corporate management sponsored an extensive survey asking employees to pinpoint critical leadership values for the 1990s. It quickly became clear that innovation was a key value, but to encourage it, a renewed focus was needed. Hence, in early 1990, DuPont chairman Edgar Woolard appointed two senior vice presidents, Bob Luft and Earl Tatum, to cochair a corporate committee. The committee had the responsibility of setting clear strategic direction and support to promote an environment that fostered creativity and innovation. The author was invited to participate because of experience gained in the divisional effort.

Initiatives of the corporate committee led later that year to the formation of the DuPont Center for Creativity & Innovation. Creativity was consciously coupled with innovation because of the recognition that creativity provides the fuel essential for innovation. The basic concept of the corporate center was to have in place a small core group that could reach out across the business units, inspiring local champions to become actively involved in learning and applying creative thinking tools in achieving successful innovations.

The Center staff included a Director (the author), a Creativity Manager (Charlie Prather), an Innovation Manager (Richard Tait), and three Creativity Associates (Helen Snyder, Theresa Kardos, and Charlene Traill), who helped administer the effort. The Center reported to two strong advocates, Alexander MacLachlan, Senior Vice President of DuPont Research and Development, and Max Pitcher, Executive Vice President of DuPont's Conoco energy subsidiary. An Advisory Board of senior executives provided added corporate support, guidance, and credibility. An Implementation Committee of middle managers helped formulate strategies and was a communication link to business units. A first step was development of vision and mission statements:

Vision:
   DuPont is acknowledged as the most innovative company in the world through creativity of people.

Mission:
   To catalyze the unleashing of the underutilized creative potential of our people, and to champion prompt implementation of best ideas to drive business success.

Strategies:
   Primary focus of the Center was:
   - **Education** of employees in the techniques of creativity and innovation.
   - **Application** of the techniques to practical problems.
   - Helping line managers establish a **Supportive Environment.**

Key components of the Center:

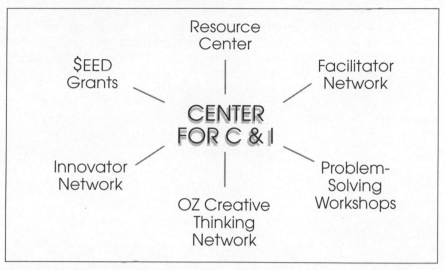

RESOURCE CENTER

A resource center was established as a focal point for communication and scheduling. Through E-mail, Creativity Associate Theresa Kardos provided information about workshops, network meetings, and news items. She also received requests for creative problem-solving workshops.

Brochure of Offerings

To publicize Center offerings, a colorful brochure was issued with descriptions of the resource center, Facilitator Network, OZ Creative Thinking Network, and $EED Program. The cover page extended this invitation to employees:

Call us when you have

- A desire to learn about creativity and innovation and improve your creative-thinking skills.

- Important business or functional problems with no easy or obvious solutions.

- Customers you would like to help with problem solving or finding new ways to use DuPont products.

- A desire to enhance the level of creativity and innovation in your organization.

- A need to interact with your community/society on issues of mutual importance, but no knowledge on how to go about it.

Resource Directory

The resource center issued a semi-annual directory that included the following: a list of available books, journals, and videos; calendar of internal and external workshops, seminars, and conferences; list of facilitators available to lead skill-building and creative problem-solving workshops; and list of seminar topics the Center staff was available to present.

Facilities

The resource center was located in the DuPont Building that houses corporate offices in downtown Wilmington, Delaware. At the time it was formed, space was limited. A wide hallway on the sixth floor with two adjacent vacant offices was selected as the Center location. A receptionist's booth was placed in a corner of the hallway. This is where Theresa Kardos set up shop with a computer station.

The hallway was converted into a library with reading tables, book shelves, and an eye-catching fish tank above which hung the Center Logo:

The fish tank and Center Logo were visible as people exited the elevator and entered the hallway, now a Creativity & Innovation Center. Creativity Manager Charlie Prather settled in one office. The other office became a video room. Center Director and Innovation Manager, Richard Tait, occupied ninth-floor executive offices, which gave status to the effort. This floor had a conference room suitable for Center meetings.

CREATIVITY & INNOVATION

CONTINUOUS IMPROVEMENT

The fish tank became a big issue. It contained live fish, and this violated building regulations. A safety inspector spotted the tank and requested that it be removed. Many employees in the area had become attached to the fish and objected. Through inaction, the tank remained without further ado. This was an example of "asking forgiveness" rather than "asking for permission," which is one of the teachings of Gifford Pinchot in creative risk taking.

Skill Building

Scheduling skill-building seminars and workshops was an important function of the resource center.

FRANK AND ERNEST · by Bob Thaves

One stream of skill building was in monthly meetings of the OZ Creative Thinking Network, discussed later in this chapter, where participants shared experiences, participated in workshops, and heard many guest speakers.

Internal workshops included sessions with professor Edward Glassman of the Creativity College on creativity tools, with emphasis on metaphoric thinking; Ted Coulson and Alison Strickland of Applied Creative Learning Systems on principles of effective thinking; and a series by Kim Barnes of Barnes and Conti on developing the creative side, intelligent risk taking, and managing for innovation. Seminars by Edward de Bono on lateral thinking and Six Thinking Hats, by Ned Herrmann on whole-brain thinking, and by Roger von Oech on creative blockbusting were always well attended. A frequently attended external workshop was Ned Herrmann's Applied Creative Thinking (ACT-I) discussed in Chapter V. Skill-building workshops were also conducted by members of the Facilitator Network.

The "Are We Creative Yet?" Calendar

As follow-up to the cartoon book described later in this chapter, a 1992 calendar cosponsored with Clay Smith, Chairman of the Corporate Marketing Committee, was issued with the theme of "paradigm busting." The cover was a Bob Thaves Frank and Ernest cartoon:

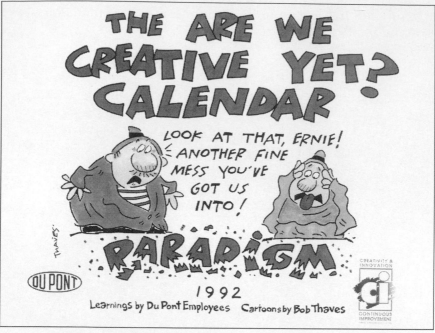

The calendar was issued to marketing managers as a vehicle to advertise the Center's offering of facilitating workshops with customers on issues of mutual interest. The back cover of the calendar describes this offering:

The DuPont Center for Creativity & Innovation offers creative problem-solving workshops in partnership with customers to tackle problems and opportunities. For further information, contact your DuPont representative or phone . . .

Each month had a cartoon to communicate a learning. For example, in December's cartoon:

FACILITATOR NETWORK

A vital function of the DuPont Center for Creativity & Innovation was to organize a network of facilitators committed to:

- Learning the skills of creative thinking
- Championing these skills across the company
- Facilitating problem-solving workshops in support of business units
- Sharing experiences to help each other grow
- Participating in a volunteer pool that the Center could call upon as needed

A charter group of DuPont facilitators met in the fall of 1990 to develop a mission statement and path forward. This session was facilitated by Jeff Nightingale, an external consultant who specializes in mission statements. Within one year, the network had over 120 volunteers from across the company. Some were full-time plant site facilitators who were versed in organizational effectiveness processes and were eager to add to their offerings. Others were middle managers wanting to learn creativity tools and processes to apply in their units. Others were front-line researchers, engineers, human resources people, and marketers aspiring to gain facilitator skills as a possible new career path. About 30–40 of the network became active, capable facilitators.

Facilitator Qualities

The success of a creativity effort depends on the quality of the facilitators. A productive workshop led by a skilled facilitator adds credibility to the value of creativity techniques and justifies the time and effort invested by participants. Success stories help spread and increase interest in creativity and requests for more workshops. A poorly led workshop endangers the entire effort.

In selecting facilitator candidates, the following qualities are important: high credibility with colleagues; motivation to "champion" creative-thinking tools and processes; good listening and communication skills; being results oriented; the ability to control group dynamics; the ability to lead the process rather than influence content; and diligence in sharing learnings and success stories.

Facilitator Training

Early in the effort, a core group of 30 facilitators spent one week in an internal workshop led by Edward de Bono. Here they learned lateral thinking tools and the Six Thinking Hats framework. Facilitators were encouraged to attend external workshops that certified them to use the materials and teach others. These included Edward de Bono's Six Thinking Hats and lateral thinking; Ned Herrmann's Brain Dominance Instrument; Michael Kirton's Adaption/Innovation Inventory; and Scott Isaksen's creative problem-solving process, Climate for Innovation Questionnaire, and facilitating CPS course.

Certification Standards

A system of standards was established where a facilitator would move to different levels of competence. Originally, there were five to ten "Master Facilitators" capable of independently leading workshops. Most of these were experienced facilitators in other fields such as organizational effectiveness and had learned the creativity tools and processes. A facilitator-in-training moved to a higher level after experiencing a certain number of cofacilitations, becoming adept at applying the creativity tools and demonstrating the qualities mentioned in this section.

CREATIVE PROBLEM-SOLVING WORKSHOPS

A primary function of the Facilitator Network was to facilitate creative problem-solving workshops for business units. This is where the creative-thinking techniques are applied to practical problems and opportunities. The creative problem-solving process and workshop design is described in Chapter IV.

Criteria for the Center to resource a creative problem-solving workshop was the following:

- High business stakes
- New direction in thinking required
- Participation of a person having decision-making authority

When a workshop request was received, an E-mail message was sent to network members asking for volunteers. High-stakes workshops justified a lead facilitator and two or three others. In most cases there would be a lead facilitator and one or two facilitators-in-training.

A responsibility of the facilitator was to share, generally via the computer network, the workshop outcome including difficulties and successful practices.

Videotaping

Videotapes of workshop segments, where participants comment on value, serve as a powerful communication tool. David Knappe, who led the video teams, was an expert in condensing videos to five- to ten-minute clips as a way to publicize the process and examples of success. Also, seminars were videotaped that could then be broadly disseminated.

During 1991, the Center administered 78 creative-thinking workshops led by 19 Master Facilitators. Many examples were discussed in previous chapters. Additional examples are described below.

Example #47

This example illustrates how a creative-thinking workshop aided a manufacturing plant in accomplishing environmental protection objectives accompanied by financial benefits.

A manager in a European plant had seen a video of a four-hour seminar given by Dr. Edward de Bono to an audience of 1,200 DuPont employees in Wilmington, Delaware. This triggered him to request that the Center facilitate a lateral thinking workshop aimed at generating ideas to improve their environmental protection program.

The workshop, led by Master Facilitator Steve Zeisler, contributed to this plant's placing 12 winners out of 475 entries for the DuPont Chairman's annual Environmental Respect Award. This plant had eliminated all raw polymer waste, totaling 485,000 pounds in 1991 in just six months. The process, according to the team, was to investigate each step that created raw polymer waste and then find a way to prevent its recurrence.

Overall, the team reduced manufacturing and waste-disposal costs by $450,000 per year, reduced the plant's energy consumption by 10 percent, and eliminated odor-related complaints from the surrounding community.

According to team members, their ability to find ways to do things differently was based upon training they had received in the lateral thinking workshop.

Example #48

This example illustrates how a creative problem-solving workshop helped provide strategic direction to a troubled business. It also illustrates the use of metaphoric thinking in developing focus areas.

A business unit was in serious trouble, losing about $1 million per month. They had exhausted the standard ideas on cost reduction, which they felt was necessary for survival. The Manufacturing Director requested that the Center facilitate a problem-solving workshop to generate new ideas on the issue:

> *How can we achieve substantial reductions in operational costs?*

The first step in the workshop was to review the history of their situation and develop possible focus areas. Master Facilitator Mary Roush used metaphoric thinking to help the group develop focus areas.

The participants were cast as a group of physicians who had a critically ill patient to treat. They each had a different specialty, e.g., a cardiologist, a neurologist, an orthopedist. The patient was the metaphor for the problem they were working on. Their job was to examine the patient for vital signs, e.g., heart failure, waste elimination, and mental problems. What would their treatment protocol be to obtain a complete recovery? Would they need to do a heart transplant, a dialysis, brain surgery, etc.?

The metaphoric output was then translated to the business situation. For example, a heart transplant would mean installing a new continuous polymerizer in the plant. This approach generated over 100 possible focus areas. Convergent thinking then led to the selection of five focus areas to carry forward to the idea generation step. Not all focus areas dealt with cost reduction.

It's difficult to judge the true impact of a single workshop on business results because so many factors are involved. Currently, this particular business is in a sound competitive position and is a good earner for the company.

Example #49

This example illustrates the importance of the design meeting in planning a workshop.

A plant was having a serious groundwater contamination problem. The estimated cleanup cost was $250 million over a five-year period. Plant management requested that the Center facilitate a creative problem-solving workshop to tackle this issue:

> *How can we remove groundwater contamination at substantially less cost and time than current estimates?*

During the design meeting in advance of the workshop, an important idea came up regarding participants. The thought was that since oil people are knowledgeable about the earth's underground, wouldn't it be of value to invite representatives from DuPont's Conoco energy subsidiary? Three people from Conoco gladly participated. Because of their presence, a breakthrough, low-cost concept for removing contaminants from the earth was conceived based on technology for removing oil from the ground.

Example #50

This example illustrates how creative-thinking tools helped generate new concepts for strategic direction of a growth business.

A business unit had put on-stream a new plant in Europe and therefore had much higher capacity than sales. The business director requested a problem-solving workshop to deal with the issue:

> *How can we grow our business faster?*

A multifunctional group consisting of marketing, technical, manufacturing, strategic business planners, and two "wild cards" convened for a three-day workshop. Many potential focus areas were identified, such as developing improved products, new applications for existing products, markets in new regions, new customers, etc.

In the idea-generation step, many implementable ideas were generated. Two examples:

- Metaphoric thinking about how we grow trees or plants led to the concept of "pruning." This led to the idea of "pruning" customers forecasted to have low growth rates. The approach was to reduce marketing and technical-service support to these customers and add them to customers with high growth potential.

- Lateral thinking generated this provocation: "Don't sell the product." This led to the concept of leasing the product and recycling, which for the products of this business was feasible.

Example #51

This example illustrates how a creative problem-solving workshop helped identify technical objectives aimed at breakthrough new concepts for a manufacturing process.

The polymer supply for a major corporate enterprise had been manufactured using basically the same process for 20 years. Ideas for major advances in process technology had been exhausted. The Enterprise Chairman requested a creativity workshop with this problem statement:

> *How can we create a breakthrough in polymer X technology to recapture worldwide leadership?*

In the design meeting, participants from across the company were identified who had scientific and engineering expertise that might bear on this issue. Criteria for success was defined by workshop sponsors as follows:

The breakthrough . . .

- Should make a big difference in the business
- Should lead us to the next step
- Should be able to lead us to pilot plant stage by the year _____

- Should be of interest to people and fit their values
- Must not prematurely limit operations

In the workshop, many focus areas were developed. The idea-generation step and convergent thinking led to new concepts for four breakthrough-type processes. As a result, resources were assigned to pursue these new concepts.

Example #52

This example describes how a workshop was used to explore ways to improve the innovation process in a business unit.

A Senior Vice President requested a session on:

How can we sponsor new initiatives and ideas in a manner that increases the success rate and does a better job of not digging deep holes?

As background, this business unit in recent years was successful at generating useful new ideas, but had difficulty taking them to market profitably. He wanted to address what this experience had taught them about the innovation process that they could apply in the future. In the workshop, many potential focus areas were identified and selected for exploration such as:

- How can we get ourselves to act on the principles and criteria that we already know are necessary to bring new products to market successfully?
- How can we acknowledge, nurture, and exploit core competencies as a fundamental building block of the business?

In the idea-generation step, led by Master Facilitator Dick Comer, the creativity techniques applied included brain writing, visual stimuli using several interesting landscape photographs, and lateral thinking. These techniques generated numerous ideas, some of which the business unit considered implementing.

INNOVATOR NETWORK

One of the challenges of the Center was to establish a company-wide network of innovators who could share learnings in creativity and innovation. To help accomplish this, the Center staff organized an event called the "Innovator Forum."

Innovator Forum

This event had this theme:

DuPont innovators accelerating the corporate vision. These were the purposes:

- Raise awareness throughout DuPont that innovation was valued and expected
- Share learnings to help accelerate commercialization of new products, processes, and best practices
- Involve and honor people at all levels in DuPont for their innovative contributions

A request for abstracts was issued with guidelines that the write-up track the innovation with a focus on basic business need; creative idea; the process of taking the idea to reality; and financial or other benefits. The "story" was to be told in a way that highlighted success factors such as creative thinking, sponsorship, supportive environment, risk taking, and overcoming barriers.

Response to request for papers was overwhelming. The Center received 265 abstracts from teams of innovators that included plant operators, mechanics, secretaries, marketers, engineers, and scientists. Essentially all business sectors, functions, and regions including Asia/Pacific, Europe, North America and South America were represented. Here is one abstract:

Is It Ivory or Is It Corian®? (Asia/Pacific) - An international ban on ivory trading severely impacted an ancient Asian art form: ivory carving. A multinational and multicultural team of DuPonters did some creative thinking and came to the aid of these carvers. This impacted the community, DuPont's corporate image, and the creation of a potentially new market for Corian®. This program has potential global impact for Corian® as a substitute for ivory, and it was also consistent with the corporate emphasis on the environment. The impetus for the entire program came about through an individual's concern for the preservation of the African elephant. This program received no direct funding from the operating department, and all of the individuals gave personal time and effort to see that it came to fruition.

Format of Forum

At one point, it was planned to have a large conference with presentations and a poster session. It was decided instead to recognize the innovators at local sites (Example #21, p. 28). This had the advantage of engaging a larger number of employees and also was more cost-effective. Site management organized these events and played a key role in publicly recognizing the innovators and their innovation, which was often the result of a team effort.

"Wave of Innovation" Award

An award having a "Wave of Innovation" theme was designed and presented to 450 innovators participating in the Forum.

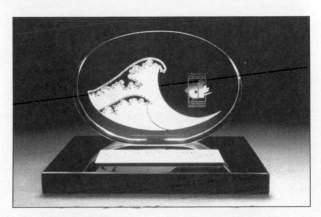

The genesis of this award illustrates the value of diversity in thinking. Originally, the plan was to use a miniature statue of Rodin's *The Thinker* as the award. This is what had been used in the Industrial Fibers Technical Division's creativity effort. Helen Brown, a member of the Innovator Forum planning team, objected to the male symbol of *The Thinker*. She was challenged to create an alternative of neutral gender and came through with the concept of a "Wave of Innovation" award. Because of her creative contribution, she was the first to receive this award.

The award was presented to 450 innovators and was accompanied by a video that presented and illustrated these words:

> *Upon a vast ocean of resources,*
> *creativity and innovation rise.*

> *A resounding, perpetual motion,*
> *pressed by the constant winds of change.*

> *New ideas rush to meet each other—taking shape*
> *and setting into motion a new wave*
> *of creativity and innovation.*

> *The wave steadily sweeps across the ocean,*
> *quickly gathering momentum and strength; improving;*
> *growing; redefining its shape.*

Soon the waves crest with the force of innovative change,
Exploding and releasing an energy that uncovers
new resources—new areas for growth and improvement.

And then, the wave quickly flows back into the ocean;
this time with a different kind of energy; an energy that will
help create the next wave of innovation.

Accelerating the Corporate Vision
DUPONT CENTER FOR CREATIVITY & INNOVATION

Forum Learnings

A summary report was issued containing these abstracts:
- Innovations in New Products and Applications
- Innovations in New Processes
- Innovations in Human Resources and Work Practices
- Innovations in Safety
- Innovations in Environmental Protection
- Innovations in Customer Interactions
- Innovations in Finance
- Innovations in Information Systems
- Innovations in Continuous Improvement

Separate reports were issued in each of these categories containing the full papers.

To capture learnings from the Forum, the Center staff wrote a series of essays in these categories:
- Needs Driven
- Teamwork
- Creative Thinking
- Diversity
- Sponsorship
- Risk Taking
- Speed of Delivery
- Continuous Improvement
- Environment for Space and Time
- Overcoming Barriers

Internal Venturers Forum

A group of new product-development managers had been meeting periodically for many years to network innovation experiences and hear guest speakers discuss topics involving taking new products to market. When the Center was formed, the Innovation Manager assumed responsibility for administration of this ongoing network.

$EED GRANTS

$EED Grants is a system that helps nurture ideas and innovation. A 1986 Innovation Audit sponsored by corporate management and administered by Gifford Pinchot led to the conclusion that the company's employees were brimming with ideas, but they needed an opportunity—and a little bit of help— to implement those ideas.

Management response to the audit was $EED, a corporate program to provide grants ranging from $5,000–$50,000 to any employee, regardless of level or function, who is committed to pursuing an idea and who needs an alternative to traditional funding sources within the company.

The grants are awarded to people with the understanding that developing the idea doesn't relieve them of current job responsibilities. It's a partnership process, with the grant providing the cash and the creator contributing personal time.

The $EED program became a responsibility of the DuPont Center for Creativity & Innovation, administered by the Innovation Manager.

CURRENT STATUS

In 1993, the creativity and innovation effort in DuPont was restructured. At that time, all training and development was contracted to the Forum Company. They assumed responsibility for portions of the Center's activities, mainly training in the skills of creative thinking and facilitation of problem-solving workshops. This is being carried out by experienced facilitators who transferred to the Forum. Many of the qualified facilitators that remain in DuPont continue to facilitate workshops in their business units.

The OZ Creative Thinking Network has remained in DuPont and continues to grow, as described in the next section of this chapter. The OZ Network of over 750 DuPonters is currently championed by a volunteer committee that organizes OZ meetings. Each meeting is sponsored by a senior executive of a business unit or corporate function.

A strong innovation effort continues in DuPont as a key element of the commitment to renewal and growth. A major program is focused on processes to reduce cycle time for delivery of new products to market. This is discussed in Chapter IX, "Taking Ideas to Market."

Overall, a renewal of creative thinking and innovation, jump-started by the Center for Creativity & Innovation, has continued as an integral part of the DuPont culture. The vital role of champions and supports is discussed in Chapter VIII.

DUPONT OZ CREATIVE THINKING NETWORK

The DuPont Company
Oz Group
Helping Others Turn Dreams into Reality

The OZ Creative Thinking Network is a volunteer group of DuPont employees devoted to educating themselves and others in the field of creativity and innovation and applying the learnings to practical on-the-job issues. This section describes how the OZ Network was organized and sustained. Also, it tells the story behind the OZ project that led to publication of a copyrighted cartoon book entitled *Are We Creative Yet?* This book pairs essays expressing concepts in creativity and innovation with Bob Thaves' Frank and Ernest cartoons.

The OZ Network is not management driven! The driver for growth over a ten-year period from 7 to over 750 DuPont employees has been a strong grassroots persistence to continue education and networking in the techniques of creativity and innovation. To accomplish this, people have dedicated quality time attending OZ meetings and sharing learnings and successes even during periods of increasing workloads.

ORGANIZATION AND OPERATION

Genesis of OZ

The OZ Network was founded in July, 1986, concurrently with the beginning of the creativity effort in the DuPont Industrial Fibers Technical Division (Chapter VI). To help plan the Industrial Fibers effort, the author invited a group of six DuPonters, knowledgeable in the creativity field, to a dinner meeting to share views about leading authorities, the literature, and "best" workshops to attend. This discussion provided excellent input in planning the divisional effort. The group included Corey Ericson, Jim Green, Jim Magurno, Charlie Prather, Tim Weatherill, and Nat Wyeth. This meeting was the first of what later became the OZ Creative Thinking Network.

The OZ name was coined in a meeting with Edward de Bono during one of his visits to the fibers division. The group introduced themselves to him as a "creativity pickup team on a bumpy, winding road toward a brighter future, as in the *Wizard of Oz.*" This metaphor stuck and led to the OZ Group name, which evolved into the OZ Creative Thinking Network. Others heard about the network and phoned to ask how to join. The only requirement was that they attend an OZ meeting. Membership grew from the original 7 in 1986 to over 750 in 1996 representing most DuPont business units and functions.

Aim

An organizational effectiveness facilitator, Hank Clark, led a process to formulate the following OZ Network aims statement:

- TO—Function as a creativity and innovation network and help enable a culture for creative thinking.

- IN A WAY THAT—Expands the company's knowledge base of worldwide concepts and technologies around creativity and innovation; continuously challenges the status quo and promotes the spirit of zealous entrepreneurship, risk taking, and unconventional approaches to problem solving; and is productive rather than time-consuming, fun rather than drudgery; and aligns our efforts with quality leadership principles.

- SO THAT—We enable people and organizations in this company to achieve and sustain a high level of innovation and commercial success.

The aim can be expressed by the "OZ Funnel," an OZ member's visual representation:

The OZ Funnel

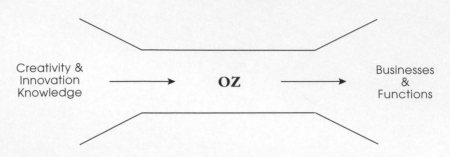

Funnel input is knowledge gathered from all sources by OZ members in the field of creativity and innovation. This knowledge is then funneled through an OZ screening. The output is creative-thinking tools and processes considered to be of value in helping solve difficult business and functional problems.

Vision

In addition to defining aims, it was important to have a vision for the future. The group adopted the vision statement of the Industrial Fibers Division:

- Creativity and innovation are valued at all levels in the organization, and management behavior consistently signals and reinforces that value.

- DuPonters are knowledgeable about the technology of creativity and innovation and are applying the skills they develop.

- DuPonters have the space and take the time to be more creative and innovative in their work.

Format of Meetings

OZ meetings are held about every six weeks. In the early years, only 20–25 members attended. They took turns around a conference table sharing experiences and learnings. If a participant had nothing to share, he or she could choose to tell a joke, sing a song, or dance a jig. This practice was suggested by

Roger von Oech, a DuPont creativity consultant. At the end of the meeting, new members received a T-shirt with the inscription:

THE OZ GROUP . . . TURNING DREAMS INTO REALITY.

This was the idea of champion Jim Green, and he implemented it. About half the group were "regulars," and the other half were new members. When attendance grew to more than 30, the sharing activity occurred in subgroups of 6–8 per table, followed by feedback to the group as a whole.

In recent years, about 150 employees have attended half-day OZ meetings, which are held at the DuPont Country Club. Some meetings have had over 300 attendees. The job level of attendees ranges from an occasional vice president to an occasional operator from a plant site, with most in between. Most business units and functions are represented. Attendance is voluntary. Some ask permission to come; others just come.

Early OZ meetings were convened by Helen Snyder, Creativity Associate, and secretary to the author. Later, the Industrial Fibers Technical Division Creativity Manager, Alex de Dominicis, assumed responsibility for the OZ Network. When the DuPont Center for Creativity & Innovation was formed in 1990, the OZ Network was convened by the Center's Creativity Manager, Charlie Prather, and administered by Creativity Associate, Theresa Kardos.

A highlight of the OZ meetings is the membership interaction with internal and external speakers who present seminars or conduct workshops on topics OZ members can use in their work. Examples of speakers and topics over the years are listed below.

Internal Speakers

Occasionally, DuPont employees have been the seminar speakers, including the following: inventors describing the creative thinking that contributed to their discoveries; innovators telling how they overcame barriers to bringing new products to market; professionals explaining the value of thinking outside existing paradigms; and people from plant and R & D sites describing "creativity teams" that meet periodically to tackle problems brought by fellow employees. Also, members of the DuPont Facilitator Network have sometimes led sessions on topics such as the de Bono Six Thinking Hats, Herrmann's Whole-Brain Thinking, Kirton's Adaption-Innovation Inventory, and metaphoric thinking.

External Speakers

At most OZ meetings, the seminar speakers are invited guests. These have included the following: Teresa Amabile on "Environment for Creativity"; Ted Coulson and Alison Strickland on "Applied Creativity"; Nils Dailey on "Managing for Innovation"; Edward de Bono on "Lateral Thinking"; Marilyn Dow on "Green Light Thinking"; Cathleen Ferguson on "Artistic Visualization"; Ken Finn and Margo Berger on "Software Lateral Thinking Assist"; Roger Firestein on "Creative Think"; Bert Freeman on "Verbal Positive Approach"; Ed Glassman on "Metaphoric Thinking"; Annette Goodheart on "Laughter and Creativity"; Steve Grossman on "Creativity Techniques"; Stan Gryskiewicz on "Creative Leadership"; Ned Herrmann on "Whole-Brain Thinking"; Scott Isaksen on "Creative Problem Solving"; Joyce Juntune on "Creativity in the Education Process"; Vara Kamin on "Value of Fables in Reawakening Our Imagination"; George Land on "Break Point and Beyond"; Leon Lessinger on "Creativity in the Florida School System"; Anthony Le Storti on "Advanced Creativity Techniques"; William Miller on "Creative Ways to Foster Continuous Improvement"; Magally Mossman on "Creative Imagery"; Kirtland Peterson on "Building the Creative Organization"; Gifford Pinchot on "Intrapreneuring"; Lee Pulos on "Creative Visualization"; Robert Purifico on "Odyssey of the Mind"; Don Reinertsen on "A Framework for Speeding Product Development"; Col. Rolf Smith on "Innovation in the Military"; Morris I. Stein on "Creativity: Fact or Fiction"; Chic Thompson on "Creativity Rules of Thumb"; Roger von Oech on "Creative Blockbusting"; and Sandra Weintraub on "Creative Problem Solving Using Dreams."

OZ Projects

The OZ Network has had several projects, including assembly of a library of pertinent books, publications, and videos; participation in an Innovation Fair honoring $EED Money recipients (Chapter VII); evaluation of creativity software programs; and publication of a cartoon book entitled *Are We Creative Yet?* This latter undertaking is the best example of a successful OZ project and is described below.

ARE WE CREATIVE YET? CARTOON BOOK

The *Are We Creative Yet?* book was created in order to communicate concepts in creativity and innovation with a humorous touch.[18] It is based on essays by DuPont employees that are paired with Frank and Ernest cartoons by Bob Thaves. The story of the book illustrates the innovation process, where a novel idea was formulated to meet a need and then taken to market.

The Idea

In September 1987, Fred Dickson, Patent Associate, attended an OZ meeting and made a presentation that addressed the OZ objective of broadly disseminating concepts in creativity and innovation across DuPont. He suggested that this could be accomplished by a cartoon book. He felt that most books on creativity were too vague, too lofty even for technical people, and not much fun.

Fred's idea for a cartoon book was triggered by this phrase in the OZ aims statement:

> . . . *to enable a culture for creative thinking and innovation in a way which is . . . fun rather than drudgery . . .*

Fred is a fan of Frank and Ernest cartoons by Bob Thaves and had noted that many of his cartoons could be related to themes in creativity and innovation. Next came the challenge of taking the idea to market.

The Idea to Market

The first step in implementation was to obtain agreement of Bob Thaves. He was supportive and enthusiastic about the project. Next, an OZ team screened 6,000 Frank and Ernest cartoons, from which 150 were selected as being pertinent to the subject. Then OZ sponsored a company-wide contest soliciting short essays from DuPont employees expressing their views on creativity and innovation that best fit these cartoons. The contest was publicized in *DuPont Directions* magazine. Kits of the 150 cartoons were provided to entrants. Winners' names would appear in the book.

Hundreds of essay/cartoon pairs were received from DuPonters in 24 U.S. states and 9 countries, from which the perceived 60 best were selected. Examples:

The Importance of Teamwork

Successful problem solvers know that what's important is to get the problem solved, not necessarily to get it solved solo. When you've come to a mental dead-end and need a better road map, leave your ego at a rest stop and ask others to help in navigating. Organize a team creativity session based on brainstorming, synectics, or other techniques. It's fun and mentally challenging. You'll be riding in the passing lane in no time.

The Importance of Gender

Some say that males are more "left-brained" and females more "right-brained." Problem-solving sessions are often more productive when there are male and female participants, possibly because of left-brain and right-brain preferences. But whatever the reason, try to include both sexes in your problem-solving sessions.

The foreword to the book has these comments by DuPont Chairman Ed Woolard:

There is plenty of room throughout DuPont for "heroes" in all types of jobs. We intend to provide "hero" status to those who show us how to get products to the marketplace more promptly and more creatively. The OZ Group's Are We Creative Yet? *cartoon book illustrates the creativity of our people and describes in a humorous vein some of the basic concepts in creativity and innovation.*

Pricing advice was obtained from the Corporate Marketing Committee. In-house printing and distribution was aided by a Marketing Communications OZ member. Agreements with the publisher of Frank and Ernest cartoons, NEA, Inc., were handled by an OZ member from Legal. Ed Woolard not only wrote a foreword to the book, he also offered help from his executive assistant to get the book published.

The OZ book idea took about three years to bring to market. The book was introduced in May 1990 at the Chairman's annual leadership meeting, where it was distributed to 400 senior executives. A large poster of this cartoon was displayed at the conference:

The Importance of Leadership

FRANK AND ERNEST ©by Bob Thaves

By 1992, over 20,000 copies of the cartoon book were either sold internally or donated to educational and nonprofit groups. The decision to sell the books rather than distribute them to all

DuPonters was made on the premise that people value something more when they pay for it.

A recognition dinner was held in Fall of 1990 for all contributors to the book. Each author was presented by two Senior Vice Presidents with a miniature statue of Rodin's *The Thinker.*

Reflections

In reflecting on this episode of OZ, there are interesting side stories. Fred Dickson was invited to join the OZ Network following his cartoon book proposal. His immediate response was typical: "I'm too busy with a high work load to attend such meetings." Yet, he attended every OZ meeting for several years until his retirement.

Many OZ members felt Fred's proposal was unrealistic because the task would require a full-time assignment, and resources were unavailable for such a project. Yet, as a team effort of eight to ten "busy" people, the job was done, illustrating the power of intrinsic motivation.

Finally, the pooling of resources from across the company was possible because the basic idea was sound, and everyone, including senior management, recognized the value of humor and creative thinking in the workplace.

FUTURE OF OZ NETWORK

The OZ Network currently operates within DuPont, administered by a volunteer committee of champions, chaired by Maria Keesling, and including Beth Davison, Dan Cornette, Scott Lewis, and Steve Scheinberg. Each OZ meeting is sponsored by a different senior executive from a business unit or a corporate function. Ongoing sale of the *Are We Creative Yet?* cartoon book at $14.90 per copy helps provide funds for seminar speakers.

In mid-1996, the OZ Network became a chapter of the American Creativity Association, a nonprofit association devoted to "promoting a creative society." The chapter chairperson is champion Bill Copish, an active member of the OZ committee.

The future of OZ depends upon the champions of OZ. These are the grassroots "core" members who regularly participate in OZ meetings despite their high day-to-day work load and apply what they learn to become more productive in their jobs. Without these champions, who have a passion for the value of serious creativity, the OZ Network would have faded out years ago. The reason OZ has continued this long is because people value creative thinking as an integral part of their lives at work and in the home.

Supporting champions are those line managers who see sufficient value in OZ to attend meetings themselves and/or enable space and freedom for people in their organizations to attend. Corporate management also deserves credit because, even during difficult economic times, they have had the wisdom to recognize that creativity and innovation is a core competency aided by the continuation of OZ.

FLETCHER CHALLENGE BUILDING PRODUCTS SECTOR CREATIVITY PROGRAM

Today, new thinking is becoming essential in business. It's the edge on the competition in terms of product development, new ways of doing business and developing better systems for serving customers.

> David Sixton, Chief Executive, Building Products Sector, Fletcher Challenge Limited

Fletcher Challenge Limited is one of New Zealand's largest companies with global operations in the building, pulp and paper, forests, and energy sectors. It is another example of a large organization structuring for creativity and innovation.

In March 1993, David Sixton, Chief Executive of the Building Products Sector, and a team of General Managers embarked on a Best Practices Study Tour to ten admired U.S. companies. This tour, organized by Tony Randall of Management Frontiers Pty Limited in Australia, was aimed at encapsulating best practice learnings under five chosen categories. DuPont was the company visited to glean best practices in creativity and innovation.

Following the Best Practices Study Tour, David Sixton established the Learning Group, headed by Claire Eeles, who became a superb champion initiating these key actions:

- Scheduling a series of seminars to educate over 1,000 employees in the skills of creative thinking. At every seminar, David Sixton introduced the speaker to visibly express top management support and expectations.

- Organizing and training a Creativity Facilitator Network of over 100 volunteers from Building Products Sector and other Fletcher Challenge business units to facilitate creative problem-solving sessions.

- Communicating to employees at all levels examples of success contributing to bottom-line business values.

- Conducting a "Creative Practices Survey" to determine areas of strength and weakness in the environment for creativity and innovation in the Building Products Sector.

- Joining the American Creativity Association to tie in with a worldwide network that shares learnings and trends in the creativity and innovation field.

CREATIVITY FACILITATOR NETWORK

The first step in organizing the Creativity Facilitator Network was to interactively formulate an aims statement that would clearly describe the purpose of the network as perceived by the sector's leaders and those people interested in being facilitators.

Aims Statement

To establish a Creativity Facilitator Network in Fletcher Challenge that is committed to:
  - Supporting the business leadership by
    - successful facilitation of value-oriented creative problem-solving sessions
    - applying the Six Thinking Hats framework to meetings and discussions
  - Promoting the knowledge and application of C & I concepts throughout the organization
  - Staying at the forefront of C & I best practices
  - Growing, supporting, and assisting each other in the Creativity Facilitator Network
  - Highlighting and recognizing C & I successes

So that we leverage the creativity of our people to gain a competitive edge.

Creativity Facilitator Training

Facilitators attended a one-day overview creative-thinking seminar to introduce them to C & I techniques and principles.

Those who were interested in learning how to lead a team through a creative problem-solving process were then signed up for more in-depth facilitator training. This included a one-day course in the Six Thinking Hats using Edward de Bono's workbooks and training materials and, for some, an Edward de Bono four-day course in lateral thinking. It also included learning a variety of other creative-thinking tools, the creative problem-solving process and skills in facilitating meetings. An important part of the training was practice in cofacilitating business-focused problem-solving workshops led by experienced facilitators.

CREATIVE PROBLEM-SOLVING SESSIONS

A primary focus of the Creativity Facilitator Network was to respond to business unit requests for creative problem solving. Examples of successful creative problem-solving sessions are described below:

Example #53

Facilitator Maree Blair from the Fletcher Wood Panels business unit reported on this session:

> *Information received from customers indicated that the edges of Melteca were cutting some users' hands. FWP had investigated a solution that required $260,000 to be spent on edge-trimming equipment. This had not proceeded as the expenditure could not be justified. However, we still had people cutting their hands, so a problem-solving team was put together to address the issue. The team decided to use creative problem-solving techniques to try to find a more economical solution.*

> *The team used several creativity techniques, including outrageous provocations, random words, and traditional brainstorming in the session. Several ideas were selected and de Bono's yellow, black, and red hats were used to determine which ideas would be implemented. The idea selected—using files (from the idea "knife steel," which came from the random word **sheep**)—has been trialled and it appears that it will be successful. This will result in capital expenditure of $1,000, a vast improvement on the $260,000 previously estimated for a solution.*

Example #54

Facilitators Clara Saville and Louise McLachlan from the

Winston Wallboards business unit reported on this session:

This workshop focused on production and sought to solve the following problem:

> *How can we maintain a minimum of 97 percent A-grade recoveries (versus current 92 percent)?*

People enjoyed using the creative problem-solving process. It's fun. People like coming up with ridiculous ideas, and more often than not, a ridiculous idea leads to a great, viable one.

Regular fortnightly follow-up meetings to the workshop assessed gain and improvements and set further targets, moving from the "creative" stage to implementation and follow-up. The involvement of a cross-section of site personnel demonstrated a commitment to the creative-thinking process, leading to the acceptance of the idea that nontraditional problem-solving methods do work and certainly help achieve results.

The 13th of September, 1994, was one of the best days we have ever had. On that day, we achieved 98.6 percent A-grade recoveries and 100 percent time utilization!! The great news is that we have kept up the standard, achieving over 98 percent A-grade recovery on standard board over the past two months.

We plan to train all Christchurch staff to use these techniques. People seem hungry for more, which is great.

Example #55

Facilitator David Garmonsway from the Plyco® Doors business unit provides this example:

The big bonus in creative problem solving is its ability to focus people's thinking. Often, that focus is enough to get people generating ideas through normal thinking patterns, but if they get stuck, the creative-thinking techniques come into play. People often think creative problem solving is for the "big issues," but it's equally useful in quickly resolving smaller problems.

We'd been going around and around in circles arguing over opening an account for a particular customer. It was the classic conflict between sales and credit control, with both looking at the customer with a different view. By using the Six Thinking Hats, we solved the problem and opened the account with slightly modified credit-control criteria. It was solved very quickly, and everyone was happy.

COMMUNICATION VEHICLES

The Building Products commitment to creativity and innovation is a key theme for the sector's communication vehicles. For example:

- Business unit leaders are expected to report on their companies' creativity and innovation activities and successes via their monthly business reports.

- The sector's *Big Picture* magazine frequently includes stories about teams' creative problem-solving efforts.

- A *Blue Hat Bulletin* was initiated to update Creativity Facilitators and other interested people on the latest creative problem-solving success stories, improvement ideas, and learning tips.

An example of a *Blue Hat Bulletin:*

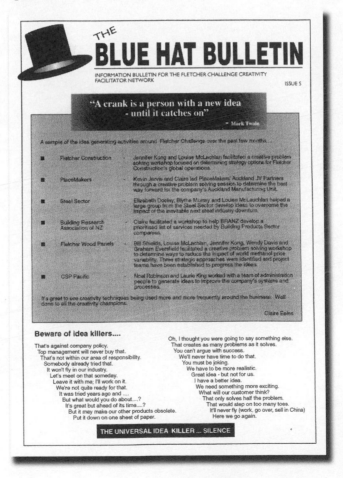

Chapter of the American Creativity Association

Fletcher Challenge Limited became the first International Chapter of the American Creativity Association (ACA). The ACA is a nonprofit, membership-driven association "promoting a creative society." Fletcher Challenge's chapter is known as "Te Ara a Maui" (the Pathway of Maui). In Maori mythology, Maui was renowned for his resourcefulness and ability to think outside current paradigms. There are many instances where it could be said that Maui made the impossible possible.

On one such occasion, while on a fishing trip with his brothers, he was determined to catch the biggest fish. However, when they refused to share their bait with him, he punched his own nose and, using the blood from it, fished up an enormous fish. This fish became known as "Te Ika a Maui" (the Fish of Maui) which, in Maori history, is the North Island of New Zealand.

THE BRIGHT IDEAS "IGNITION FUND"

While the creativity effort in Fletcher Challenge was centered in the Building Products Sector, other sectors in the company were introduced to creativity and innovation techniques and principles via the Creativity Facilitator Network and creative problem-solving workshops. After being exposed to the Building Products Sector's Best Practice Study Tour learnings, Fletcher Challenge's Concrete Sector introduced a Bright Ideas "Ignition Fund," championed by General Managers John Illingsworth and Keith Avery.

The Bright Ideas "Ignition Fund" was promoted in Keith Avery's PlaceMakers business unit as a way to encourage employees to suggest "big step" improvement ideas. Keith appointed a full-time Vision Coordinator to educate employees about the company's vision and help them develop their ideas and provide resources needed to give these bigger ideas a chance. A booklet was designed to help communicate the Bright Ideas concept:

The booklet states, "The Vision Coordinator at Support Office can help make the most of your ideas by talking with your manager about your idea to ensure that you get the support that you need to develop the idea; helping you plan the project and work out timetables and milestones to ensure that the project is successfully managed; finding technical help or any other kind of 'expert' help you may require; and if money is required to develop the idea, the Vision Coordinator can help arrange this through the Bright Ideas Ignition Fund."

The booklet also describes the process for submitting the idea, how it is processed, and how employees will be recognized for their improvement suggestions. To date, well over 50 "big step" improvement ideas have been submitted with several translating into major, implementable cost-saving initiatives and market-development programs.

CURRENT STATUS

The Building Products Sector of Fletcher Challenge continues to champion creativity and innovation as a mechanism to continually improve. The sector's largest company, Fletcher Wood Panels, uses huge creative problem-solving sessions (where everyone at a factory site is invited) to involve people from all levels of the company in solving business issues.

Fletcher Wood Panels is also using creative-thinking techniques to identify industry breakthroughs as part of the company's "Re-Creating FWP" business process reengineering efforts.

Throughout the Sector, the key elements of a successful/impactful program are in place and building momentum:

- Strong leadership from Chief Executive David Sixton, Claire Eeles, and the sector's business managers.

- Keen champions in each business unit to maintain a strong focus on using creative problem solving as a business-improvement tool.

- An enthusiastic Creativity Facilitator Network, spread throughout the business units, on a faster-than-usual learning curve, gaining valuable experience in facilitating creative problem-solving sessions and achieving meaningful successes.

- A large pool of talented people eager to learn and apply creative-thinking tools in their everyday work.

The challenge for the future will be to maintain continuity in fostering a supportive environment where people feel free to take risks in trying new things and where applying the tools of creative thinking becomes even more of a part of the sector culture at all levels in the organization.

The Fifth Dimension: Recognizing Emerging Champions and Supports

The key to gaining and sustaining momentum for a creativity and innovation effort is the sprouting and blossoming of local champions. Off-site management can set the tone, but the effort takes hold when on-site managers and individuals on the front lines become energized practitioners and leaders.

A creativity champion, in the context of this book, is an individual who becomes convinced of the value of creative thinking techniques and actively applies these to practical issues. The productive champion realizes that creativity is a means to an end, is results-oriented, and leads by example, striving to inspire others to learn and apply these techniques. Many champions have been highlighted in prior chapters, particularly in connection with examples of practical application of creative-thinking techniques.

Most champions described in this book became initially motivated by exposure to an Edward de Bono seminar on lateral thinking, Ned Herrmann's Applied Creative Thinking workshop, a Roger von Oech creativity seminar, Gifford Pinchot's Innovation Audit, or the other events described in prior chapters designed to provide a supportive environment. Attendance at OZ Creative Thinking Network meetings seeded many champions.

A way to engage potential champions is to provide feedback cards at the end of a creativity seminar where attendees can request information on how to join a creativity network. For example, in October 1990, a half-day lateral thinking seminar by Edward de Bono to an audience of 1,200 DuPonters generated over 200 such requests. This was a factor in step-change growth of the OZ Creative Thinking Network.

Credibility on value of creative-thinking techniques increases manifold when people observe respected colleagues taking the initiative to learn and apply creativity techniques. This was the case with Jean Prideaux, an exemplary champion.

EXEMPLARY CHAMPION

Jean Prideaux was Technical Group Manager, Kevlar®, at the Richmond, Virginia, plant site heading up a group of 15–20 R & D people. A mechanical engineering Ph.D., Jean immediately grasped the potential of learning and applying creative-thinking techniques. Stimulated by site creativity seminars and external workshops, he became a passionate creativity champion. He led by example, industriously applying creativity learnings to practical issues in his own and adjacent programs. This helped motivate both technical and manufacturing people across the site to learn and apply creativity techniques. The following two examples are typical of Jean's contributions.

Example #56

This example illustrates the true meaning of "learning and applying."

Jean Prideaux attended an off-site Roger von Oech creativity workshop where he and five others were asked as a group to organize a skit designed to sell a new product. They were given only six minutes to do this, which seemed like an impossible task. Surprisingly, under pressure, they did a good job. When Jean returned to the plant, he wondered how he could apply this type of "creative stretch" in setting and accomplishing technical objectives.

The opportunity to apply "creative stretch" came when Jean's group met to set annual objectives to improve manufactured polymer uniformity, crucial in spinning a high-quality Kevlar® fiber. The previous annual goal of 5 percent improvement was difficult to achieve. Jean suggested that the goal be a 50 percent improvement. The group was stunned, feeling that this was an impossible task. He asked why. The response was "To do that, we would have to do this . . . ." This type of "stretch thinking" set in motion a program that, as Jean put it, "failed miserably . . . the group achieved only a 40 percent improvement." The following year they achieved another 25 percent on top of that. The savings from this accomplishment was $6 million annually. This episode was portrayed on a videotape that helped others understand the value of creative thinking and contributed to ongoing momentum.

Example #57

This example describes a joint effort with the Kevlar® manufacturing group that Jean's group interfaced with. Together they won the first annual "Chairman's Environmental Respect Award" in 1990. Approximately 1,000 applications were entered for the award describing progress in environmental protection from sites across the DuPont company. These were reduced to about 200, from which the Kevlar® accomplishment was selected.

The Kevlar® accomplishment was based on a broad-based attack on hazardous waste that reduced process waste in the polymer area by over 80 percent. The creative steps to protect the environment also saved the business $3 million annually. The manufacturing cochampion of this effort, Group Manager Larry Tolpi, wrote the following:

> *Many of the efforts undertaken by the Kevlar® team members were considered or attempted in the past without success. One of the reasons they were successful this time is that over the last several years, Kevlar® has had a program to change the environment for creativity and innovation and to give the organization the skills necessary to do their jobs more creatively. These are exactly the kinds of results hoped for.*

Jean Prideaux took the initiative to promote creativity across the entire plant site. He helped structure, with consultants Ted Coulson and Alison Strickland, a local creativity workshop called POET (Principles of Effective Thinking), which was offered to all site employees. He initiated the ACT-I alumni group described earlier, was an ardent member of the OZ Network, and became an effective facilitator for creative problem-solving workshops. He published a "joke of the day" via E-mail to the OZ and Divisional Networks that started each day with a smile.

Jean was recipient of the first "Creative Leadership" award presented at a staff meeting attended by his colleagues and accompanied by thunderous applause. He was truly an exemplary champion.

Exemplary Cochampion

A cochampion was Jean Prideaux's secretary, Bonita Bailey, to whom Jean referred as his "superstar." On her own initiative, Bonita decided to convert her office into the "Office of Innovation." She organized a library of creativity books and videos that were available to all employees. She tracked and posted relevant news items and schedules for seminars, workshops, and conferences. She assisted Jean in issuing the "joke of the day." She set an excellent example for other support people to participate in the creativity and innovation effort.

Emergence of a New Champion

Sometimes an individual is touched by a personal experience that illustrates the value of creative thinking and leads to the emergence of a new champion. Such was the situation with Steve Borleski, Technical Group Manager, Divisional End-Use Research. Steve was not sold on the value of creative-thinking techniques until an experience occurred at home over the weekend that made him a believer and an active champion.

Steve's wife had asked him to fix their vacuum cleaner, which had become clogged and inoperable. This was a centralized system that networked throughout the house. Steve assumed the system was clogged somewhere in the network and painstakingly crawled through the piping areas searching for the problem—to no avail. He told his wife to hire a serviceperson. She refused, responding, "With all that creativity training going on at work, you ought to be able to solve this problem."

Steve sat down on the floor, leaned against the wall, and began to think. He reminded himself of a basic principle in creative thinking, i.e., before acting on the first idea that you perceive to be the solution to your problem, review the alternatives. He mentally did this and realized that in his haste he had failed to look at the most obvious place . . . the vacuum cleaner nozzle. He did so and solved the problem. On Monday morning, he came to work a firm believer in the value of creative-thinking techniques.

Some readers may snicker at this example as being unbelievable. Yet how often have we rushed into a wasteful action only to realize in hindsight how obvious the solution was if only we had taken the time to think through alternatives?

As a result of the vacuum cleaner incident Steve became an active champion, urging his group to apply creative problem solving in tackling difficult issues needing new direction in thinking. Many examples emerged from his group over time, including the application of creativity techniques in design of an improved bullet-resistant Kevlar® vest for the military.

SUPPORTS

A creativity support is a person who encourages, enables, and protects creativity champions in their pursuits. Creative supports are essential in helping create a supportive environment and in the sprouting and blossoming of champions. Creativity supports are generally middle and upper management, who recognize the vital role of creativity in paving the road to innovation. Some people are both champions and supports.

Support from top management is vital. Sometimes it emerges unexpectedly. Such was the case when Ed Woolard, DuPont Chairman, offered unsolicited help in publishing the OZ Network cartoon book *Are We Creative Yet?* The author had made an appointment with Mr.Woolard to describe the book and ask him to sign a foreword based on comments he had made about the importance of creativity and innovation. He glanced through the book, read the foreword, and signed it. He kept the draft copy. The next day, his executive assistant, Elizabeth Browning, phoned. She said that Mr. Woolard had shown her the cartoon book and suggested that she help speed publication. Needless to say, this support from the Chairman helped successfully bring this creativity and innovation project to reality.

Another example of top management support was the determination of David Sixton, Chief Executive of Fletcher Challenge Building Products, to introduce and apply creative-thinking techniques across his business sector. His initiatives are described in Chapter VII.

There were several key supports that contributed to success of the Industrial Fibers effort described in Chapter VI. An exemplary support was Dick Reese, Vice President of the division, who unequivocally supported the author in initiating the creativity effort. Chad Holliday, then Business Manager of Kevlar®, was particularly responsive to incorporating creative-thinking techniques into the Divisional businesses. The efforts of champion Jean Prideaux in Kevlar® R & D, as described above, were strongly backed by unit heads Ted Sandukas and Murray Brockman.

Supports for the DuPont Center for Creativity & Innovation and the OZ Creative Thinking Network are discussed in Chapter VII.

An example of a person who is both strong support and ongoing champion is Franz Ehrhardt, a senior executive in DuPont's Conoco energy subsidiary. Franz was on the Advisory Board of the Center for Creativity & Innovation, became skilled in creativity techniques, and is often called upon by colleagues to facilitate problem-solving sessions when a new direction in thinking is required.

Support for creative thinking doesn't necessarily require that people learn creativity techniques, although they are helpful. Mike Emery, Business Director of Tyvek® at the time, created an environment for creative thinking in his organization by publicizing the slogan "Dare to Be Different." His concept was that being willing to be different in a constructive way would lead to being better. The only constraints imposed were that the action be legal, moral, and safe. An example that illustrates his approach is described below.

Example #58

A marketing rep in Mike Emery's organization visited a customer to react to a complaint. The rep concluded that the complaint was valid. He took out his wallet and paid the claim. He charged it on his expense account. The accountants yelled "foul." Emery had a party to acknowledge his "daring to be different," giving status to this act and reinforcing the environment for creative thinking.

The Sixth Dimension: Taking Ideas to Market

Coauthored with Richard H. Tait*

Ralph Waldo Emerson once wrote:
  Next to the originator of a good saying is the first quoter of it.

Extending this thought to the context of this chapter:
  Next to the originator of a good idea is the first to recognize its value and do something about it.

Prior chapters have been concerned mainly with creativity, the generation of novel, useful ideas. Good ideas are wasted unless brought to market. This chapter is concerned with taking ideas to market, which is our definition of the innovation process. The chapter includes an innovation overview, several case histories of successful innovations, and a section on Product and Cycle-Time Excellence (PACE)—a structured framework for making a step-change improvement in managing new product innovation.

INNOVATION OVERVIEW

Innovation has been defined in many ways, all having certain elements in common:
- "The process by which knowledge is developed and applied in new ways to the needs and material operations of society." (Peter Drucker)
- "To create and bring into profitable commercial use new products, processes, and businesses." (Gifford Pinchot)
- "The process of bringing any new problem-solving idea into use." (Rosabeth Moss Kanter)
- "A battle in the marketplace between innovators or

---

* Richard H. Tait, Ph.D., was Innovation Manager, DuPont Center for Creativity & Innovation and, more recently, Senior Consultant, DuPont Continuous Business Improvement. Currently, he is President, R. H. Tait Associates.

attackers trying to make money by changing the order
of things and defenders protecting existing cash
flows." (Richard Foster)

- "An innovating organization is one committed to
  renewing itself." (H. Smith Richardson)
- "Putting into effect something that is new."
  (Edward de Bono)

While creativity is mostly an individual effort, innovation is
usually a team effort. It is not just one simple step, but an
integrated process of creative steps that yields the defined goal.
Innovation is important in all functions, including marketing,
manufacturing, R & D, finance, and human resources. It is
usually, but not always, triggered by "market pull" vs.
"technology push." Successful innovation requires involvement of
both the producer and user of the new idea or concept.
Innovation may be viewed as occurring in one of three time
frames:

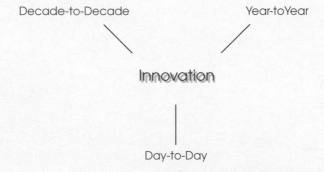

Decade-to-Decade innovation involves commercializing entirely
new businesses such as Kevlar® aramid or step-change new
processes like Conoco's tension leg platform for oceanic oil
drilling. Year-to-year innovation involves major shifts in existing
businesses, such as introducing new products like DuPont
Stainmaster® carpets or an advanced new pesticide. Day-to-day
innovation involves contributions to constructive change on a
daily basis from people at all levels in the organization. All three
types of innovation are critical to the future health of business
and industry. Similar innovation time frames hold true in other
fields, including education, government, communication, social
sciences, and the arts.

INNOVATION PROCESS

The innovation process generally involves these steps:

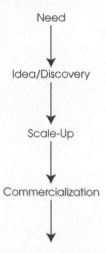

Needs-Driven Innovation

FRANK & ERNEST® by Bob Thaves

The first step in the innovation process is definition of a market
or workplace need. This need triggers an idea or a discovery.
Next is demonstration that the idea or discovery meets the need.
If successful, this is followed by scale-up and commercialization.
By commercialization, we mean bringing the idea to reality. This
includes not only breakthrough ideas, but day-to-day ideas. For
example, it could be a salesperson getting a creative idea on how
to meet a customer need and implementing it, or an engineer
with a creative idea on how to double throughput of a process
and accomplishing it, or a secretary with a creative idea to
improve office efficiency and doing it.

Bringing an idea successfully to market, particularly in the decade-to-decade or year-to-year time frames, requires three core elements working together: (1) the innovation team; (2) leadership sponsorship; and (3) the innovation road map. The team provides the horsepower for doing the work. The leadership ensures support, strategic guidance and an ongoing supply of resources. The road map lays out the path for the team to follow. When properly structured, these elements will reinforce each other and accelerate the rate of progress. The leadership effectively staffs the team. The team continually upgrades the road map. The road-mapping process prepares the leadership to supply resources to the team at critical moments.

Each of these key structural components has special features and dynamics that must be attended to for the overall innovation process to function well.

INNOVATION TEAM

The innovation team is formed to plan and carry out all the tasks to take an idea from concept to commercialization. This team encompasses both the small, close-knit group of people at the heart of the innovation effort and the broader group of people that they call on for help.

FRANK AND ERNEST by Bob Thaves

OKAY, WE'VE GOT 100,000 INFANTRY, 20,000 CAVALRY, 35,000 ARCHERS AND 150 CATAPULTS. ...NOW WE NEED TO THINK UP A CATCHY SLOGAN.

In organizing and managing teams for successful and rapid innovation, there are three critical requirements:

- Ensuring that the team includes the right people at the right time to deal with the full array of tasks and issues. This includes assembling people with a diversity in thinking styles and preferences (Chapter V) as well as the required expertise and experience.

- Ensuring that the selected people are effectively chartered and empowered by the sponsoring leadership to take actions as required so that their work is both timely and on target.

- Ensuring that the team has a well-structured internal managing process to coordinate their activities.

For new product innovation, it is common practice to recruit the core technical, marketing and manufacturing people early. Unfortunately, the perceived "less critical" support people, such as the product safety experts, the raw materials supply team, or the community relations resources, are often engaged too late in the effort. In addition, team members are often given only limited guidance and authority so that frequent "checking in" is required, which stymies progress. Even when a new product team is appropriately staffed and chartered, it will frequently struggle to make progress because of misaligned actions.

McGrath, Anthony, and Shapiro have described how to use a structured "core team" with a supporting "project team" to drive rapid cycle time in new product innovation.[37] The core team leads and coordinates the total program and has well-defined roles and responsibilities for each team member. It has an appointed leader and clear guidelines on how it will function as a team. The support team provides the resources and power to complete the myriad tasks required for successful commercialization. Individual core team members are assigned to see that the effort of each part of the support team are systematically integrated into the overall effort.

The core team/support team approach is as effective for innovation in general as it is for new product development. It provides a powerful framework to convene the key capabilities needed for implementation of an idea. The power of this approach is its ability to help a team and its sponsors to systematically organize the team's communication, decision-making, and work-planning processes and to systematically integrate/coordinate all the disparate work-streams that constitute the innovation effort.

When the right people are correctly teamed, empowered, and "clicking together," the innovation process works remarkably well, as illustrated in the case histories described later in this chapter.

LEADERSHIP SPONSORSHIP

Sponsorship is the process that ensures the innovation team gets the ongoing support, resources, guidance, and "protection" it needs to move forward.

Sponsorship is not a "hands off" leadership process. Sponsorship involves the leadership team:

- Rolling up its sleeves to help the innovation team work through its issues and talk through its plans

- Setting a strategic vision and spending time with the innovation team to help them "see themselves" in that vision

- Helping the innovation team organize for success and supporting them when they hit difficult times

- Setting the tone that challenges the team to think and innovate broadly

- Listening to the team and working with them to ensure an effective ongoing dialogue that keeps them energized and consistent with organizational needs

Sponsorship is not a "blank check" process. It involves the leadership:

- Making choices and acting on them

- Consciously deciding to build the resource base that fully meets the needs of the innovation initiative, but in a way that is cost effective

- Expecting the innovation team to set and meet milestones, expecting them to focus their efforts where the true value for the organization lies

- Challenging the team to be clear, honest, and up-front about problems and issues so that together they can resolve them

- At times, helping the team see that the direction they are taking should be dramatically shifted

A lot has been written about the importance to an innovation effort of having an individual leadership sponsor. Yet, what the innovation team needs often goes beyond a single individual. At times, one person can control all the resources and have the authority needed to provide effective sponsorship, particularly for small-scale innovations. However, there are many more situations, especially in large corporations, where one person simply does not have the capability, authority, or "political clout" to fully empower the innovation team, despite his or her best intentions.

The resolution to the sponsorship problem lies in constructing a comprehensive sponsorship process. Such a process should enable the leadership to identify the individual building blocks of sponsorship needs and to systematically assemble and link them for each innovation project. A challenge for the leadership of organizations that want to institutionalize innovation is to devise a system that does not rely on individual sponsors but creates a robust sponsorship capability that can support the full portfolio of innovation initiatives.

Someone has said that "Innovation is not an academic exercise . . . it is a people exercise." At its heart, sponsorship is simply the part of the "people exercise" linking the organizational leadership and the innovation team. The goal is to establish a linkage that enables the team and the leadership together to make the right decisions and take the right actions to drive the innovation forward.

INNOVATION ROAD MAP

The "Innovation Road Map" is the structured path the innovation team takes to move from idea to market. The key to rapid and successful innovation is to develop this road map early in the innovation journey. In this way, the team knows from the start what tasks must be completed and what resources will be needed. With the road map in hand, the team's energy can be devoted to working on critical tasks rather than continuously struggling with the question of "What do I do next?"

In building the road map, the goal is to identify the steps that must be successfully completed, to systematically organize them into a logical sequence, and to set up a framework for follow-through, with agreed-to milestones. This up-front planning is essential to ensure that the team effectively handles all the work-streams necessary for commercialization. This includes specifying and optimizing key technologies, developing and implementing needed operational processes, structuring and managing critical interactions with the marketplace, and building the organization needed for sustained performance.

The Innovation Road Map must constantly be reviewed and updated to deal with unexpected contingencies, since things do not always go as planned.

NEED FOR PLANNING

The Three Core Elements Integrated

All three core elements—the team, the sponsorship, and the road map—need to be in place and functioning for successful innovation. Too often, rough going is encountered when one of them is omitted. For example:

- The innovation team may be committed to drive forward. But without the full support of the organization leadership, its chances of being "resourced to win" are usually very slim.

- The leadership may fully back an idea. But without a clear road map for taking the idea to market, the team's likelihood of success is dramatically reduced.

- The Innovation Road Map may be crystal clear. But if a strong team is not in place to implement it, then progress can stall.

While all three core elements are essential, it is not always necessary that they be consciously installed. There are examples of successful innovations in which these elements were "intuitively" implemented. However, insightful organizations realize quickly that they can't rely on chance or intuition if they want to systematically capture the marketplace value of their portfolio of creative ideas. They realize that they must install structured innovation processes and systems and institutionalize these. The commitment to consciously building organizational capacity and capability around the innovation process differentiates long-term marketplace winners from losers.

When all three core elements of the innovation process are in place and running smoothly, the rate of progress in bringing ideas to market can be dramatic. This is illustrated by the examples described below.

INNOVATION CASE HISTORIES

In previous chapters, many examples of the Day-to-Day type of taking ideas to market were described, where an individual or group generated a creative idea and quickly implemented it. For example, Floyd Ragsdale's idea of how to solve the collapsible hose problem and demonstrating it the following morning, Example #14, p. 23.

This section describes examples of successful innovations of the Decade-to-Decade and Year-to-Year type: Kevlar® aramid fiber, an entirely new business venture; DuPont Stainmaster®, which revolutionized the residential carpet industry; CFCs replacements to meet the environmental ozone challenge; crawfish bait, where a two-man team bootlegged an idea that led to a profitable new business; and a process for Product and Cycle-Time Excellence.

The driving force and road map for taking each of these ideas to market were quite different, but many of the basic principles and learnings about the innovation process are common to all four. The examples are DuPont innovations where the authors have firsthand knowledge or were able to draw from others who do.

KEVLAR® ARAMID FIBER

Kevlar® is a lightweight, high-strength, manmade organic fiber which, pound for pound, is five times stronger than steel. Applications include bullet-resistant vests, fireblocking fabrics, sails, ropes and cables, and reinforcement of tires, brake linings, and high-performance composites in aircraft.

The story of Kevlar® provides a perspective of what is involved in taking a laboratory discovery to the reality of commercial production. The Kevlar® innovation story began in the early 1960s when DuPont management identified a need for the next-generation high-performance fiber. The ensuing research and development program yielded an important scientific discovery in 1965. In 1972, a one-million-pound-per-year market development plant was built. By 1982, full commercialization was reached with a 45-million-pound-per-year plant.

During the period from discovery to commercialization, several reality gaps and tough hurdles had to be overcome. The Kevlar® innovation described below illustrates the importance of multidisciplinary teams, consistent leadership sponsorship, and close surveillance of the innovation road map, where many changes were required because of unexpected events.

The Kevlar® innovation also illustrates the value of an environment that encourages creative thinking, risk taking, and questioning conventional wisdom. Several publications provide a detailed technical description of the Kevlar® innovation.[38–40]

The Need (Early 1960s)

The invention of nylon and subsequent fibers provided DuPont with a direction to continually find better fibers. In the early 1960s, DuPont research management envisioned a need for a superfiber with the heat resistance of asbestos and the stiffness of glass:

Envisioning the Need

The Idea/Discovery (1965)

The route to achieving goal fiber properties was perceived to be through stiff chain para aromatic polyamides, a class of materials expected to have unusual properties. The idea seemed sound, but previous attempts to spin these materials into fibers had been unsuccessful because of their extreme insolubility and intractability. Overcoming these barriers to "test" the idea became the basis of a research program.

A breakthrough occurred in 1965, when Stephenie Kwolek, a research scientist at the DuPont Experimental Station in Wilmington, Delaware, prepared a watery, opaque solution of an aromatic polyamide polymer that could not be clarified by heating or filtration. Conventional wisdom implied that the solution had too low a viscosity to be spinnable into fibers and that the opaque solution had very fine suspended particles that would plug the spinneret holes. Had Kwolek followed conventional wisdom, Kevlar® may not have been discovered. The fascinating story of what happened next is told by Gene Magat, Research Manager responsible for the research effort:[38]

> *The procedure at that time was to give the polymer solution to an experienced technician in charge of the spinning unit, and he would spin the solution. The technician required clear solutions. Furthermore, he objected to the low viscosity of this polymer solution, saying that "it flowed like water." He refused to spin it. Yet crude spinnability tests by Kwolek, such as dipping a spatula in the solution and lifting it, gave a steady flow of polymer solution just like honey. Quite a different behavior from forming droplets if it were a "water-like" solution. In spite of its strange appearance, she insisted on having it spun. The polymer solution spun into fibers without any difficulties. The as-spun fibers had amazing properties.*

We now know that the solution opacity was due to the formation of polymer liquid crystals, not suspended particles. This material had never been prepared before. The liquid crystals had shear-oriented in the spinneret capillaries, enabling surprisingly good spinnability.

Demonstration (1965–1970)

When the fibers were sent to the physical testing laboratory to measure properties, the reaction was total disbelief. Maybe a mistake had been made! The fiber properties of this first aramid fiber tested was startling! The physical test laboratory had to rerun it several times before anyone would believe the results. The fiber had extreme stiffness—four times greater than glass— and a breaking strength many-fold higher than existing fibers.

The stress-strain curve that measures fiber strength and stiffness is shown below for Kevlar® vs. other fibers:

Kevlar® Properties vs. Other Fibers

The first reality gap was soon encountered. The raw materials that were used to demonstrate the concept were too costly to justify scale-up. A major program was launched to understand the physical chemistry of liquid crystalline solutions. With that knowledge, a suitable polymer was developed from lower-cost ingredients. This polymer, called PPD-T, eventually became the basis of Kevlar®. Things looked promising as the ingredient costs were reasonable and the product properties were unique.

The second reality gap quickly showed itself. The spinning solvent had to be 100 percent sulfuric acid, yielding solutions that were too viscous to spin at economical speeds. Hence, the process was impractical. This became starkly apparent when the researchers first described the invention to the manufacturing and engineering people who would have to design, build, and run the plant. They didn't want it!

The concern about the sulfuric acid spinning solvent was that it was unconventional and highly corrosive. Also, spinning process yields and throughput were very low, and investment was very high. These are the realities that research people don't pay much attention to when they are at the frontiers of discovery.

A major breakthrough came when another DuPont research scientist, Herb Blades, went against the conventional wisdom that PPD-T polymer would be degraded by sulfuric acid at high temperatures. In all prior research, mixing and spinning procedures were carried out at about room temperature. Instead, Herb heated the polymer solution containing the 100 percent sulfuric acid to elevated temperatures. Unexpectedly, the PPD-T polymer and sulfuric acid did not degrade, but formed a crystalline complex. This discovery, coupled with new spinning technology, enabled much higher polymer concentrations than previously possible and dramatically improved spinning economics.

The manufacturing and engineering people became receptive to the sulfuric acid challenge when they understood the new process, the stakes, and became members of the "core team." Now the development was ready for scale-up.

Scale-Up (1971–1972; 1973–1977)

The next reality gap, of a significantly different kind, involved moving the development from the laboratory to a plant site. At this point, it was particularly important to coalesce a multidisciplinary team.

Translation of a laboratory discovery to a practical, scaleable commercial process is one of the hardest tasks faced by a technology-driven industry. In the case of Kevlar®, a new business unit was formed and a task force of dozens of scientists and engineers of many disciplines was assembled. Some of the researchers in the laboratory in Delaware moved to the plant site in Virginia. The task was to develop the manufacturing basic data and tackle scale-up.

In less than two years from the laboratory discoveries of Blades, Kevlar® was being shipped to potential customers from a one-million-pound-per-year market development plant. Considering the complexity of the process, this timetable was rapid. Five years later, the product was being produced in a 15-million-pound-per-year market development plant.

Several hurdles during scale-up were encountered. How was the spent sulfuric acid to be disposed of after spinning? This was solved by converting it into calcium sulfate (gypsum), which is useful to wallboard and cement manufacturers.

Another problem involved the unexpected finding by DuPont Haskell laboratories, in a lifetime exposure study with rats, that the polymerization solvent, hexamethylphosphoramide, was an experimental animal carcinogen. Immediate steps were taken in the handling of this solvent to be certain that there was no hazard to the workers, the community, or the customers. To avoid using a potentially hazardous material, a crash technical effort was mounted that identified an alternative solvent.

Throughout the scale-up phase, there was an underlying confidence and enthusiasm in the multidisciplinary teams. There was no hurdle that couldn't be jumped, although at times it took considerable energy, creative thinking, and unfailing support from the leadership to do so.

Commercialization (1982)

Thus far, the reality gaps in moving the program along and the hurdles in scale-up to a market development plant have been described. An equally difficult challenge was to demonstrate the market potential of Kevlar®. This was necessary to justify the final step in the innovation process . . . a full-scale commercial plant requiring a $400 million investment. Hence, throughout the development, there was intensive parallel effort to find practical applications for this new fiber. For Kevlar® to be a commercial success, sufficient value-in-use had to be found versus incumbent fibers such as nylon, steel, fiberglass, and carbon, to warrant a pricing structure that made economic sense.

Early in the development, it was recognized that Kevlar® was a unique fiber that would not automatically fit into existing applications. This became apparent from initial evaluation in tires, ballistics, composites, ropes, cables, asbestos replacement, etc. Each application had to be viewed as a "system" requiring a systems approach. *Fortune* magazine referred to Kevlar® as "a miracle in search of a market."

A "systems" engineering approach required the combined talents of people from many disciplines. Early partnerships with customers was vital to success. The "systems" approach to product development with several examples is described in a paper entitled "Kevlar—from Laboratory to Marketplace through Innovation."[39] The story of how two end-use researchers bucked conventional wisdom and developed a special form of Kevlar® to replace asbestos in rubber reinforcement markets was discussed in Example #19 on p. 26.

Today, Kevlar® has more than 200 applications ranging from surgical gloves to racing boats to tennis rackets to industrial belts, ropes, and cables. In its applications of lightweight body armor, Kevlar® has saved the lives of over 1,800 police officers who were shot in the line of duty.

For her invention of Kevlar®, Stephanie Kwolek was inducted into the United States Inventors Hall of Fame. In August 1996, President Clinton awarded her the National Medal of Technology, the government's highest technology honor.

Learnings

There are several key learnings from the Kevlar® innovation history. It exemplifies the kind of hurdles that must be overcome, and the interdisciplinary teams and sponsorship necessary to overcome them, in order to bring a laboratory discovery into commercial reality.

The management set clear objectives on the need for a next-generation fiber and defined a well-founded general approach to meet the need. This led to a focused, productive research program.

A laboratory environment for creative thinking and risk taking enabled researchers to challenge conventional wisdom. This led to breakthrough technologies that sparked development and enabled forward progress.

Rapid scale-up to a market development machine was aided by several factors: highly motivated, success-oriented people and multidisciplinary teams; consistent top-management support; an organization structured as a new business unit, separate from existing businesses; and transfer of technology by transfer of people.

Full commercialization was prolonged, not only because of the huge investment required, but because most of the applications for which Kevlar® was suited, e.g., tire reinforcement, ballistics, high-performance composites, etc., were life-supporting, which generally takes five to ten years of prove-out.

Early partnership with customers was essential to define product "fit," especially since Kevlar® properties were unique and required "zero base" applications thinking. Commercialization could have been faster by entering into partnership with customers during the early laboratory demonstration phase rather than later in the development. The barrier to doing this was the concern of exposing proprietary technology too early.

Finally, this case history illustrates that taking breakthrough technology to market successfully requires all three of the innovation core elements discussed earlier in this chapter: innovation teams; leadership sponsorship; and an innovation road map.

DUPONT STAINMASTER® CARPETS

This example of "taking ideas to market" describes how an innovation team revolutionized the U.S. residential carpet industry.

DuPont commercialized nylon in 1939 and has continually pursued new uses and improved product performance. In wall-to-wall carpeting, nylon has been the high-performance material of choice since the late 1950s. Competition in this area has exploded since the early 1960s, requiring that DuPont make a step-change in the speed of market introduction of new products to stay competitive.

The DuPont Stainmaster® story is an example of the power of a capable and impassioned team to rapidly bring an idea to market. This innovation is one of the Year-to-Year variety and built on DuPont's strength in nylon technology innovation that had been nurtured in the decades since nylon's discovery. However, the competitive environment was extremely challenging in 1986, the year Stainmaster® was introduced. A strong commitment to speed in taking the innovation to market was vital, or the opportunity could have been captured by another company.

The Need

In 1983, DuPont did a series of market studies to define what customers were looking for when they bought carpeting. An important finding was that consumers placed high priority on soil and stain resistance. Over the years, DuPont and its competitors had developed several technologies to help hide soil. However, while there had been many attempts to develop ways to reduce staining, no significant progress had been made.

The Discovery

In early 1985, research chemist Armand Zinnato walked into John Hesselberth's office with two carpet test samples demonstrating a step-change improvement in nylon stain resistance. John, who was then Technical Director of DuPont's carpet fiber business, immediately recognized that he was looking at the makings of a revolution in the residential carpet industry. What Zinnato had uncovered in a "bootleg effort" was technology that could dramatically improve stain resistance of nylon carpet fibers. As he listened to Zinnato's presentation, John realized that taking the concept to market would be a major challenge. It would require significant change, not only in the way the fiber was manufactured, but also in the way the carpet mills converted that fiber into carpet. John recognized that the potential of the new technology was huge, so he committed himself and his R & D organization to seeing it through to full implementation.

Demonstration and Scale-Up

If R & D people had been assigned to move the concept forward without the early involvement of other functions, then the story of this innovation would not have turned out as it did. For the commercialization of Zinnato's discovery, which became DuPont certified Stainmaster® carpet, was clearly a multifunctional and multiorganizational team effort. The willingness of senior management to assign people from all key areas to the innovation team, to give them clear guidance on where to head, and then to empower and fund them to act, was central to DuPont's ability to beat the competition in the marketplace. John Hesselberth has said, "The critical item was the team we built—they were all energetically committed to making it happen."

The word of Zinnato's breakthrough spread through the DuPont Fibers Department, creating excitement around the initiative. People quickly volunteered to be part of the program. Within months of Zinnato's initial "show and tell," a market launch team had formed, primarily by self-selection, and had begun to drive the program toward rapid commercialization. The project core team had representatives from marketing, manufacturing, R & D, product management, and technical marketing. It was led for most of its life by Bob Axtell, then Business Manager of Residential Carpets. Their fundamental charter was to beat the competition to the marketplace. This was a major challenge since there were hints that some competitors were hot on the trail of similar leads. The challenge was met by merging the demonstration and scale-up phases into one continuous effort in order to meet the target of a September 1986 launch.

The team met regularly to coordinate the multiple workstreams that were moving in parallel. The tasks ranged from fully defining the technology to organizing the carpet mill certification program and implementing new fiber processing operations in the plants. It also included structuring a high-impact consumer advertising campaign and planning the retail marketplace interface. The team quickly expanded its scope beyond the boundaries of the Fibers organization. They established working relationships with the DuPont Chemicals and Pigments Department to bring in specialized know-how on stain- and soil-resistant chemicals, and with the advertising firm BBDO, which created the award-winning TV commercial used to kick off market introduction.

While the core team played the central coordinating role, everyone involved saw themselves as part of the Stainmaster® team and did their part to keep the program on-track. The powerful vision of what the product could do in the marketplace was a unifying, electrifying force that kept everyone focused. The strong capabilities of the people working on the project enabled them to drive forward without a lot of back-tracking and stopping to "check in."

The innovation core team saw all the pieces falling into place as the launch date approached, but not without a struggle. Repeatedly, the team had to marshal its resources to address problems around the technology, the market interaction process, and timing. A good example of what they faced was the program with the carpet mills. The need to bring scores of different carpet manufacturing mills up to speed on the new technology and to get them certified to meet DuPont's standards in time for launch was a major challenge. As John Hesselberth said: "Sometimes it seemed that we were just one step away from disaster." But as with elsewhere in the program, the right people were put on the task and given the right support and the right direction to deal with the problems as they came up. Bob Shellenbarger, the lead technical person for the mill program, was given free rein to do whatever he saw necessary to deal with key issues. At one critical point, Shellenbarger was assigned exclusive use of a corporate jet so he could be wherever he was needed, whenever he was needed there.

Commercialization

The multitude of pieces being handled by the broad-based support team, with the core team still managing the whole, all fell into place at the right time. DuPont's announcement of Stainmaster® was followed rapidly by Allied-Signal's announcement of Anso-V Worry-Free® carpet and Monsanto's announcement of Wear-Dated® carpet—both with stain-resistant properties. But Stainmaster's high level of performance, its well-planned market launch, and its extensive and superbly executed advertising strategy took the U.S. carpet industry by storm. By the end of 1986, Stainmaster® was well ahead of its competitors in brand awareness. At the winter carpet shows in early 1987, 78 percent of new styles introduced by the mills were Stainmaster®. Through the rest of the decade, Stainmaster® was one of the largest DuPont earners. Currently, Stainmaster® still holds the largest share of the branded U.S. residential carpet market and continues to have the highest name recognition among consumers.

Learnings

There are many learnings from this story: the importance of building the right innovation team; the critical need to "resource the team to win"; the value of working with all the right parties; and the empowering effect of a clear and powerful vision of the future. But there was one major lesson that many involved reinforced—the pivotal role that senior management sponsorship played. John Hesselberth commented: "Without the support of Tom McAndrews, the Flooring Systems Division Business Director at the time, this whole thing would never have happened." McAndrews sponsored the team, lobbied with Corporate Management and effectively "sold" the program, including the radical and pivotal concept of a multimillion-dollar consumer advertising campaign. In the end, it was McAndrews' sheer will and determination that energized the program and sustained it through to its successful conclusion. This theme— the role of senior management—is also seen in the next innovation story.

CFC REPLACEMENT

In the early 1930s, Kinetic Chemicals, a DuPont and General Motors combine, pioneered the wide-scale commercial introduction of a class of chemical compounds known as chlorofluorocarbons, or CFCs. These new materials, also known as Freon® (DuPont's trade name), were developed to replace hazardous chemicals then being used in refrigerators and air conditioners. CFCs were extremely safe to handle and soon became the refrigerants of choice worldwide.

After World War II, creative people began to discover a range of new uses for these unique materials. Consumption grew, and by the mid-1970s, more than 1.5 billion pounds were being produced annually by more than a dozen companies worldwide, with DuPont being the single biggest producer.

In the early to mid-1970s, concern began to develop about the environmental impact of CFCs on the earth's stratospheric ozone layer. Over time, the importance of halting production of these materials grew clearer. In the end, DuPont realized that it had to take the lead to completely curtail production of fully halogenated CFCs.

The innovation team met the challenge and beat the original phase-out commitment by several years. There were a number of key drivers for the success of this effort, including clear goals, a strong team, the full commitment of top management, and, most importantly, a plan for implementation of the key discoveries.

Phil Meredith, then Freon Products R & D Director, has said: "The up-front planning we did was very comprehensive—we really worked hard to do it right up-front."

The Need

Through the mid-1980s, evidence for the atmospheric buildup of CFC decomposition products and their possible role in ozone depletion continued to accumulate. In 1986 and 1987, DuPont took the leadership to sponsor the development and signing of an international agreement to limit growth of CFC alternatives. This agreement—the Montreal Protocol—called for a near-term "freeze" in production and consumption and then a reduction over time to an appropriate "safe" level. Meeting these requirements represented a significant challenge to the Freon® Products Division of DuPont. Major creative thinking was needed to develop and phase in the commercialization of CFC alternatives. The challenge looked doable and the team set out to make it happen, ramping up the development program for alternative materials.

In 1988, the "need" changed radically. In March of that year, a NASA study group issued the first consensus executive summary report directly linking fully halogenated CFCs with a measured decrease in the Antarctic stratospheric ozone levels during the Antarctic springtime. Within ten days of that report, DuPont had reassessed its position and publicly committed to a total phase-out of CFC production with a complete conversion to new alternatives. The initial commitment was to complete CFC phase-out no later than the turn of the century. But as more data accumulated, the leadership realized that the target date needed to be more aggressive. They challenged the Freon® team to dramatically accelerate the schedule. The team stepped forward, committing to a full transition to replacement materials by the end of 1995.

The Discovery

Publication in the 1970s on the CFC ozone depletion theory had stimulated research on new replacement materials. Basic concepts on alternatives were in hand by 1980. Promising substitute chemicals had been identified and synthesized. Creative concepts on manufacturing processes as well as product-safety and product-use knowledge had been developed, but work to discover the best manufacturing processes was still needed.

Beginning in 1986, as new data on ozone depletion came in, DuPont reenergized its research program. The company further accelerated the effort in 1988. A series of key discoveries were made over the next several years, mostly focused on chemical manufacturing processes that were critical to meet the 1995 pull-out date.

Demonstration and Scale-Up

The pull-out commitment was a "big time" challenge to the creativity and innovation capability of the organization. The time to develop and broadly commercialize new large-scale processes in the chemical industry is very long—routinely more than a decade for complex and creative new technologies. The CFC replacement program was all that and more. The technologies for making and using these materials were new and unproved beyond the initial research and pilot work. Major new manufacturing facilities would have to be designed and built to incorporate these innovative chemical process technologies. The wide-scale marketplace conversion of existing user systems, in particular the large installed base of air conditioners and refrigerators, would require dedicated support. Many of the new compounds would have to undergo critical safety testing. This entire complex transition effort would have to be effectively organized and coordinated to ensure that the multitude of individual pieces came together in the proper sequence to meet the target replacement date.

The Freon® Products innovation team accepted the challenge. The leadership put together a comprehensive and integrated road map of all the work that had to be done to fully demonstrate and scale-up new technologies. They staffed the effort focusing on technology and engineering to support the design and development of new facilities. But they also included marketing and technical service to support marketplace conversion and public affairs to support interaction with the community and governmental bodies. They mapped out the work, established a clear timeline, and secured the backing of top management. Importantly, the support teams were chartered to go out and make it happen.

Demonstration and scale-up succeeded beyond expectations. By mid-1988, the designs for major demonstration pilot facilities were complete. By early 1989, these pilot plant facilities were started up at the company's Ponca City, Oklahoma, plant. These facilities allowed the team to demonstrate key technologies in exactly the same mode of operation as the commercial facility. This enabled the team to catch critical process problems early and to develop plans to address them before the commercial plant started up. The pilot plant also served as a supply point for the large quantities of material needed for safety testing. As Joe Glas, Vice President and General Manager, DuPont Fluoroproducts, has commented: "The key to our successful commercial start-ups were our fully integrated pilot plants."

Commercialization

By late 1989, all key elements were in place to support construction of commercial facilities. The technology-transfer process was effectively managed, and construction of the first plant went exceedingly well. The first plant, which is among the most technologically innovative projects in the chemical industry, was up and running in December 1990, six months faster than most comparable DuPont projects. The second and third plants came on-stream shortly thereafter. In late 1993, the fourth plant, with a major increase in capacity and still more new technology, was up and running. By the end of that year, the toxicity testing of key materials was completed with good results, and the program to establish marketplace conversion technology was well in hand. All the pieces of the commercial introduction program fell into place. The introduction and testing of these new chemical-process technologies and materials was so rapid and effective that the schedule was further accelerated and announcement made that a full CFC phase-out would occur by the end of 1994.

Although DuPont was ready to complete CFC phase-out by year-end 1994, the U.S. government requested that the company continue CFC production until the end of 1995, because the rest of the country wasn't yet ready for the transition. For its efforts, DuPont received the EPA's Atmospheric Ozone Protection Award, as did several individuals in the Freon® organization.

Learnings

There were many reasons for the success of this innovation. One that stands out is the emphasis placed by the innovation team in careful and in-depth planning. Road mapping was high priority throughout the life of the program starting with the technology. The team systematically thought through the key pieces of technology that had to be developed and put in place structured programs and plans to test and evaluate them.

Another place where detailed planning played a key role was in the creative design and construction of the four new facilities now operating. A systematic approach was road-mapped for development of well-defined specifications and basic data, detailed integrated network plans, and proper sequencing of the tasks. Clear principles and guidelines for effective project execution were committed to up-front and followed. For example, no design work started without completed basic data. Construction units built the facilities without change. These techniques allowed the construction program to be completed quickly and within budget.

Like the experience with Stainmaster®, a critical success factor was the innovation team itself, an empowered and excited group that stayed intact throughout the entire critical period. In describing how the people worked together, it is probably better to talk about the many teams that were in place, since well-structured teams were established in many key areas. These were teams on the pilot facilities, teams on individual plant projects, teams on the user conversions, etc. Their work was coordinated from the top of the organization, but each one clearly knew its tasks and was given the freedom to act without having to continuously "check in." Phil Meredith commented, "We assumed everyone was doing his or her job, so we didn't have to meet all the time." They were an enthusiastic and committed bunch. As Tony Vogelsberg, lead public affairs person on the team, said, "There was an esprit de corps that was unbelievable."

Another significant factor was that innovation was taking place concurrently in many places. Innovation on a small scale was encouraged throughout the broader effort and became the standard for the whole team. For example, the approach to the toxicity program broke new ground. Joe Glas knew that this effort would be expensive and time-consuming, so he and his team planned a creative approach to address that challenge. They organized all major CFC producers worldwide to form and fund PAFT—the Program for Alternative Fluorocarbon Toxicity Testing. This organization was chartered to plan and carry out a systematic program to determine the potential health effects from the new compounds. This was the first time that a major worldwide industry had voluntarily undertaken the cooperative testing of the safety characteristics of new compounds. The program was effectively staffed and met the timeline commitments to support wide-scale commercial launch.

Another example of targeted innovation within the broader effort was the technology used in the fourth plant. The challenge for the research team was to discover creative ways to utilize existing CFC plants in order to lower new investment. Innovative technologies allowed the company's CFC plant in Japan to carry out a key process step enabling significantly more capacity for the same investment than key competitors.

Most of those involved in the program keep referring to the same key point made in the Stainmaster® story—the critical role played by senior leadership. They repeatedly say that leadership sponsorship and support was an essential element in success. Leadership at the highest levels continuously asked how they could assist. They did almost no "second guessing" and looked at themselves as "helpers," not judges. But it was not a "blank-check" support. Management was actively involved and continuously challenged the team to be creative in getting the most bang from each buck of investment. With senior management behind them, acting as true encouragers while at the same time expecting the best from everyone, the innovation team felt empowered and capable of dealing with everything they faced.

CRAWFISH BAIT

The crawfish bait innovation illustrates many basic principles of how to take an idea to market, but in a somewhat different way than the prior examples. It is a fascinating story, described in a picturesque DuPont video, of how two production employees bootlegged an idea that led to commercialization of a new product. A series of subsequent events led to the purchase of the technology by the inventors, who have formed their own company, and are applying the technology, among other things, as part of a package to control rabies.

The story features DuPont production worker Jay Daigle and chemist Mal Smith. The original focus of their innovation was crawfish, which for hundreds of years was a primary food source for people of French Canadian heritage living in the bayous of Louisiana. Many continued to live close to the water, where fishing and trapping was a way of life and income. In recent years, the popularity of crawfish and the Cajun way of cooking has spread nationwide. Cajun restaurants have sprung up in many locations. Patrons can enjoy the flavor of a culture as much as the flavor of a food. All of that had led to a huge demand for crawfish.

The Need

Besides being a production worker, Jay Daigle raised crawfish on the side. This part time business was meant to be a relatively effortless source of additional income. But there was a problem—none of the available crawfish bait lasted long enough to make setting the traps worthwhile. Daigle commented, "There were artificial baits in the summertime, but they only lasted for a few hours. In the wintertime, the only bait was fish, but it was hard to handle and had many disadvantages." There was clearly a need for a long-lasting crawfish bait.

The Idea

Daigle had an idea that an inert polymer matrix might make the bait last longer. He took his idea to his friend Mal Smith, who was a chemist, and they began bootlegging some experiments. They tested the samples at Daigle's crawfish farm. The results were encouraging, so they continued their pursuit of an improved bait. They realized that because of the polymer, which was not water soluble, they could provide crawfish farmers with a bait that would disappear only when the crawfish ate it. This increased bait life dramatically, from several hours up to as many as seven days. They talked with farmers who were enthusiastic about the concept. Smith commented, "Everyone wanted it . . . we had a market crying for something that we could provide."

Demonstration

At first, the project was kept under wraps. Smith and Daigle borrowed time from other projects to develop their long-lasting crawfish bait. Smith commented: "There was an odor in the back of the lab, but everybody looked the other way. I'm sure that our supervision knew we were doing something, but we were never asked." Daigle commented: "By their turning their heads, it gave us the opportunity to do something before we asked for some money."

The innovators finally told people about their project. At first, people said it wouldn't work. The Plant Manager said that they had invented the wrong thing. But when they explained their concept and its advantages, people offered help and volunteered to join the team.

The team's basic philosophy was that if they had a good product, they ought to get it into the marketplace as soon as possible. Smith felt that if the product meets the need, it would be best to refine it in the marketplace rather than in the laboratory . . . that the reason many products don't reach the marketplace sooner is that they are "tested to death."

Smith and Daigle went to the Agricultural Products Department for help, but they were turned down because crawfish bait didn't fit into their product line. It was up to Smith and Daigle again to find their own way to market.

The team decided that the best approach was to make some of the bait and give it away to farmers to try in their traps and compare with other products. The trials were a success. The farmers wanted the bait and wanted it badly. It created suction in the marketplace. The farmers called on the Agriculture Products marketing people requesting information about availability. Now the Ag Products people called on Smith and Daigle for help in producing and selling the crawfish bait.

Scale-Up and Commercialization

The giveaway was a huge success, and farmers came back for more, but crawfish bait was just the beginning. It was commercialized by DuPont as Aquabind® and sold into other markets such as a binder in shrimp feeds.

The technology and rights were purchased from DuPont by the two innovators who formed their own company, Bait-Tech. Applications for the technology have been expanded. For example, it is now being used as part of a package in France and some regions of the U.S. as a way to control rabies.

Learnings

The crawfish bait innovation is an example of an individual having an awareness of a clear market need that could not be filled by competitive products. He generated an idea to meet that need and formed a team with another person who had the expertise necessary to explore and demonstrate the idea.

A "permitting" environment enabled the team to bootleg the project. It was kept quiet until the team had confidence that the idea would work and that there was a market for the product. They refined the product in the field rather than in the laboratory.

The innovators did not give up, even though the project had been turned down because the product didn't fit into the established business. They "warriored" for their idea to keep it alive. In this case, they created suction for the new product by taking it to the marketplace, sampling potential customers. In the process, they leveraged the company's image to add credibility to the development.

Finally, the concept started small, but bloomed into a potentially large opportunity. While the technology was developed for a long-lasting crawfish bait, it found application in an entirely different end-use, namely, the control of rabies.

PRODUCT AND CYCLE-TIME EXCELLENCE

In recent years, DuPont has undergone a major transformation in the way it develops and commercializes new products. Starting in 1991, business leaders began implementing a disciplined process called PACE—Product and Cycle-Time Excellence[37]—to create a step-change improvement in product development performance.

The PACE story demonstrates that the innovation process itself can be the target of innovation. The process can explicitly be structured and systematically organized to successfully take a continuing stream of ideas to market. Further, it illustrates the role that a dedicated champion can play in supporting the process.

The Need

The ability to rapidly bring high-value new products to the marketplace that satisfy customer needs is critical for a company to successfully compete in the long term. Companies that are leaders in product innovation are routinely winners in the marketplace. During much of the last 60 years, DuPont has grown significantly through introduction of major new product offerings, beginning with nylon. However, by the early 1990s, the company was no longer the clear leader in new product introductions. Other companies were outperforming DuPont in many critical areas. The management recognized a clear need to reshape the way the company brought a new product to market.

The DuPont effort to institutionalize an improved product development process began in earnest in 1989 when the company set out to benchmark the "best in class" in new product innovation. A team was formed and fanned out across the globe to identify the "best practices" used by world leaders.

They returned with some definitive answers:
- Business and functional leadership must be fully involved in the product-development process.
- Multifunctional product-development teams that are effectively organized and staffed with dedicated team leaders are critical.
- Structured development methodologies that are well understood and systematically used are a must.
- Key customers and suppliers need to be systematically integrated into the effort.

The study team concluded that implementing these practices across the company had the potential to significantly improve the aggregate business performance.

The best-practices study stirred a lot of dialogue about whether and how to act on these learnings. There were two nagging questions: (1) how could improvement efforts be ensured to yield sustainable organizational change; and (2) how could a process be put into place to yield a continuing flow of high-value new products—not just a few individual successes. It was important to escape the corporate "program of the month club" approach in order to create a lasting impact. Many times the businesses had tried to upgrade their product development processes, but often they wound up in another unused manual. The company needed to go beyond isolated successes and move to a process that didn't depend on the sheer will and determination of individuals. The innovation process clearly needed to be transformed, but in a way that would yield sustained business value.

The Discovery

The path taken to apply the benchmark learnings was to bring PACE to the company. The PACE process, created by the consulting company Pittiglio, Rabin, Todd, and McGrath, was an innovative approach to new product development that the benchmark team had seen in action at another company. PACE incorporated the key elements needed for an effective innovation process:
- Core teams to manage individual projects
- Senior management program approval committees (PACs) to provide consistent multifunctional sponsorship
- Business-specific structured development methodologies and guidelines for the teams to use as a road map

- A disciplined phase-review process to bring the teams and leadership together for clear "go/no-go" decision making

The above key elements were designed to be mutually reinforcing with a PACE manager, drawn from a business, trained to provide ongoing resourcing and oversight.

PACE brought something in addition to these structural elements—i.e., a creatively crafted approach to implementing these innovation process elements in a business in a lasting way. This installation methodology includes an up-front diagnostic of key issues. It focuses on systematically training and developing the organization, with extensive emphasis on leadership behaviors, to address these issues. The installation process helps everyone, particularly senior business and functional management, to clearly understand the role they are expected to play and allows them to "practice" their roles. Detailed guidelines and systematic roll-out of the process help institutionalize the process. One of DuPont's PACE implementers has said, "What is really unique about PACE is not the process itself but the way it is implemented."

Demonstration and Scale-Up

PACE had already been tested and demonstrated at several companies by the time DuPont considered it. Still, most business management had a "show-me" attitude and wanted to see it demonstrated internally before applying it in their organizations. Two of DuPont's business directors—Jerome Smith of Diagnostic Imaging and Mike Bowman of Advanced Composites—agreed to spend the time, energy, and money to implement it in their operations.

From this small beginning in 1991, the process has systematically moved across the company to cover an ever-widening range of strategic business units (SBUs) and development projects. The key corporate champion for the process was Eric Shuler, PACE Initiatives Manager, who played a major role in this wide-scale adoption. He led the "sales" effort with the business leadership to overcome the barriers to acceptance. He secured the sponsorship of the Senior V.P. of R & D and was the first member of the Corporate PACE Team. He brought in key people from the PRTM consulting firm to help begin implementation. He established a PACE Network to help support early adopters and played the pivotal role in building internal capability to implement the process.

Commercialization

By 1996, about two-thirds of DuPont's SBUs had implemented this corporate best practice. Others are applying its key principles to their own development processes. The company has a fully functioning corporate PACE team as part of a Continuous Business Improvement internal consulting group. All PACE implementations are resourced by in-house consultants. Currently, there are more than 200 major development programs being managed using the PACE framework with a cumulative projected NPV exceeding $2.5 billion.

Results from use of the PACE framework have been significant. The comprehensive alignment of the development activity and the business strategy that the PACE process establishes has allowed many businesses to more effectively target their development dollars. In addition, the ability of the businesses to respond to marketplace/customer needs in a timely manner has improved substantially. The businesses using PACE have routinely seen 30–50 percent improvements in cycle time across the entire development portfolio with 70-percent improvements in some selected areas.

For one DuPont organization, the business results have been particularly striking. Before PACE was introduced, that business was reaping very little from its investment in new product development. Less than 15 percent of its revenues were coming from new products launched in the previous three years. Following the full roll-out of PACE, that performance dramatically improved. Today, that business derives more than 75 percent of its revenues from new products. The business has gone from introducing just a couple of new products every year to introducing a stream of eight to ten new ones each year. All of this has happened despite a 40-percent reduction in R & D funds available for new product innovation.

Learnings

The vital role of a champion was clear. Eric Shuler's efforts to persuade senior management to broadly apply the methodology was pivotal in the rapid spread of PACE.

The actions of senior management have been critical to the success of PACE. Corporate management designated PACE as a best practice and supported the establishment and funding of the PACE team, but did not mandate that the businesses adopt it. By not mandating the process, senior management avoided the corporate program "rejection" syndrome and allowed the businesses to recognize the value. Corporate management knew that sponsorship for adopting the process needed to come from the leadership of the businesses, since they would have to "own it" for it to work.

Another key factor is the role that business and functional leadership played in making the PACE process function in their respective businesses. PACE provides a structured framework to engage them in decision making so that they truly provide sponsorship for the product innovation teams in their organization. By ensuring that the leadership is fully trained and supported in their role as sponsors, PACE ensures that successful product innovation is not a "onetime" process.

The PACE process in DuPont has become such a powerful engine for excellence in product development that it is now a subject of intense interest by customers and other companies doing benchmark studies. What interests them most is DuPont's ability to have fully institutionalized the PACE process for new product innovation. This institutionalization is a truly distinguishing feature.

Summary

Total Creativity in Business & Industry focuses on the practical application of creative-thinking techniques and a road map to building a more innovative organization. The book is based on the author's experiences as Director, DuPont Center for Creativity & Innovation, and R & D Technical Director, DuPont Industrial Fibers Technical Division. Programs for "total quality" were in place, but building a more competitive innovative organization required effort on "total creativity," since creative thinking fuels innovation. Total creativity requires attention to six discrete dimensions in creative thinking, described in Chapters IV to IX and summarized below.

The book contains 58 examples of how creative thinking has been applied to practical issues. Some illustrate how a particular creativity tool led to an actionable idea. Others illustrate how such ideas resulted from normal thinking patterns in a supportive environment. Some show how frameworks like the Six Thinking Hats and the creative problem-solving process is applied to tackle difficult issues. Many examples quantify the impact on earnings improvement and setting of strategic direction. Thirty-one Frank and Ernest cartoons by Bob Thaves add a light touch to a serious subject.

Chapters I–III

These chapters overview creative thinking as a skill and the value of creativity in problem solving, innovation, and quality improvement.

Creativity, in the context of this book, is the generation of novel, useful ideas. *Innovation* is the taking of best ideas to market. Innovation is the pay-off, but will not occur without the generation of novel, useful ideas. Successful problem solving is likewise reliant on creative thinking. *Creative thinking* is a skill that can be learned and improved upon even for those who do not perceive themselves as being creative. Regardless of the skill level a person might already possess, he or she can always hone that skill, just as in any sport or activity by learning and applying creativity techniques. The field of creative thinking can be viewed as encompassing six important dimensions.

The First Dimension (Chapter IV)—Learning & Applying Creativity Techniques

This chapter describes 18 productive creativity tools, processes, and frameworks with 37 examples of practical application.

In tackling difficult issues that require new directions in thinking, it is often necessary to step outside normal thinking patterns. There exists systematic, deliberate, proven tools that help us do this, such as lateral thinking, metaphoric thinking, and capturing and interpreting dreams. There also exist useful processes that help collect ideas within our normal experience base such as brainstorming, mind mapping, and brain writing. Excellent frameworks are available that help focus our thinking effectively, such as the Six Thinking Hats, the Creative Problem-Solving Process, and Synectics.

The Second Dimension (Chapter V)—Valuing Diversity in Thinking

While creative-thinking skills are key in successful problem solving and innovation, another important component is diversity in thinking.

Frameworks to measure an individual's thinking preferences and creativity style have been well documented. Examples include the Herrmann Brain Dominance Index and the Kirton Adaption-Innovation Inventory. These provide valuable inputs when organizing problem-solving workshops and innovation task forces. While style and preference influence an individual's situational behavior, there are other characteristics that impact performance. For example, creative thinkers and doers have an absolute discontent with the status quo, seek alternative solutions to problems, have a "prepared" mind, and have an intense interest in what they are doing.

The Third Dimension (Chapter VI)—Engaging the Organization

To sustain a productive creative-thinking effort, it is essential to become part of the culture rather than a program that will soon wane.

A supportive environment helps energize an organization to learn and apply creative-thinking techniques. Creating a supportive environment for creativity and innovation is like any culture change. It takes time, patience, and consistency to achieve lasting results. People generally resist change and new time-consuming programs. Therefore, to engage the organization, it is best to just start doing certain things, particularly educating people in the tools of creative thinking in a natural, nonthreatening way. A culture-change model was helpful in creating a supportive environment in the DuPont Industrial Fibers Division. The model has four components: giving status to the effort; putting in place certain routines; rewarding and recognizing individual and team efforts; and defining taboos that inhibit risk taking and the creative process. Frameworks exist that measure the environment for creativity and innovation that help engage the organization and track progress. Inventiveness and patent filings soar in a creative environment

The Fourth Dimension (Chapter VII)—Structuring for Creativity and Innovation

Structures and systems are vital in organizing for enhanced creativity and innovation.

Formation and operation of the DuPont Center for Creativity & Innovation and the Fletcher Challenge Building Products Sector creativity effort had these key elements: visible, ongoing support by top management; a central core group to strategically plan and implement the effort; operation of a two-way communication network to publicize skill-building offerings and receive requests for help, particularly in attacking high-stakes business issues; a competent group of facilitators who are well grounded in the skills of creative thinking and facilitating creative-thinking sessions; and a system for tracking and reporting examples of success.

Organizing a creative thinking network of grassroots supporters who intrinsically value creative thinking is a way to ensure an ingrained base constituency to carry on in case other structures or systems fade. An example is the DuPont OZ Creative Thinking Network of volunteers devoted to educating themselves and others in the skills of creative thinking. This group of over 750 members is completing its tenth year of operation administered by a devoted group of champions. A successful OZ project was the 1990 publication of a book entitled *Are We Creative Yet?* This book communicates concepts in creativity and innovation by pairing essays by DuPont employees with Bob Thaves' Frank and Ernest cartoons.

The Fifth Dimension (Chapter VIII)—Recognizing Emerging Champions and Supports

The key to gaining and sustaining momentum for a creativity and innovation effort is the sprouting and blossoming of champions with management support.

In a creativity and innovation effort management can set the tone, but the effort takes hold when individuals on the front line become energized practitioners and leaders. A creativity champion in the context of this book is an individual who becomes convinced of the value of creative-thinking techniques and actively applies these to practical issues. The productive champion realizes that creativity is a means to an end, is results-oriented, leads by example, and inspires others to do the same. An exemplary champion is described in this chapter, as are many others throughout the book. Equally important to the effort are creativity supports who are generally middle and upper management who recognize the vital role of creative thinking in paving the way to innovation. They "protect" the champions and contribute to the supportive environment.

The Sixth Dimension (Chapter IX)—Taking Ideas to Market

Good ideas are wasted unless taken to market, which in the context of this book is the innovation process.

The innovation process involves defining a need, generating an idea or making a discovery that meets the need, demonstration, scale-up, and commercialization. The innovation process has three time frames: Decade-to-Decade, involving launching entirely new businesses; Year-to-Year, involving major shifts in existing businesses; and Day-to-Day, involving contributions to constructive change on a daily basis from people at all levels in the organization. All three are critical to the future health of business and industry. Bringing an idea successfully to market, particularly in the first two time frames, requires three core elements working together: the innovation team; leadership sponsorship; and the innovation road map. Five examples of successful DuPont innovations are described, ranging from Kevlar® to crawfish bait.

Appendix—This section contains: (A) an index of the 58 examples of practical applications described throughout the book; (B) 19 creativity and innovation networks and centers with which the author is familiar; and (C) selected readings that might be helpful in continuing one's education.

Appendix

A. EXAMPLES OF APPLIED CREATIVITY

B. EXAMPLES OF DUPONT INNOVATIONS

C. NETWORKS AND CENTERS

This is a list of networks and centers with which the author is familiar. Most publish periodic newsletters and convene annually or semiannually.

- Advanced Practical Thinking Training, Inc.®
  10520 New York Avenue
  Des Moines, IA 50322
  515-278-5570; FAX 515-278-2245

- Alden B. Dow Creativity Center
  Northwood University
  3225 Cook Road
  Midland, MI 48640
  517-837-4478; FAX 517-837-4468

- American Creativity Association
  Box 2029
  Wilmington, DE 19899-2029
  302-239-7673; FAX 302-234-2840

- Association for Managers of Innovation—
  Center for Creative Leadership
  3859 Battleground Avenue
  Greensboro, NC 27410
  910-545-2810; FAX 910-288-3999

- Center for Creative Leadership
  3859 Battleground Avenue
  Greensboro, NC 27410
  910-545-2810; FAX 910-288-3999

- Center for Creative Learning
  4152 Independence Ct.
  Sarasota, FL 34234
  813-351-8862; FAX 813-351-9061

- Center for Creative Studies
  P.O. Box 901
  Gwynedd-Mercy College
  Gwynedd Valley, PA 19437
  215-646-7300

- Center for Studies in Creativity
  Buffalo State College
  1300 Elmwood Ave, Chase Hall 244
  Buffalo, NY 14222-1095
  716-878-6223; FAX 716-878-4040

- Creative Education Foundation
  Creative Problem Solving Institute
  Union Road #4
  Buffalo, NY 14224-3402
  716-675-3181; FAX 716-675-3209

- Creative Problem Solving Group—Buffalo
  1325 North Forest Road—Suite 340
  Williamsville, NY 14221
  716-689-2176; FAX 716-689-6441

- Georgia Studies of Creative Behavior
  183 Cherokee Avenue
  Athens, GA 30606
  706-543-9679; FAX 706-353-7247

- Humor and Creativity, The Humor Project
  Saratoga Institute
  Saratoga, NY
  518-587-8778

- Innovation Network
  34 E. Sola Street
  Santa Barbara, CA 93101
  805-965-8477; FAX 805-963-8220

- Inventure Place
  National Inventors Hall of Fame
  221 South Broadway Street
  Akron, OH 44308-1505
  216-762-6565; FAX 216-762-6313

- Kirton Adaption–Innovation Network
  Occupational Research Center
  Highlands, Gravel Path
  Berkhamsted, Hertfordshire, HP4 2PQ, UK
  44-442-871-200; FAX 44-442-871-200

- National Center for Creativity, Inc.
  17 West Market Street, Suite 980
  Indianapolis, IN 46204
  317-639-6224; FAX 317-639-6225

- National Inventive Thinking Association
  P.O. Box 836202
  Richardson, TX 75083
  214-871-5806

- Network to Improve Thinking and Learning
  597 Hill Avenue
  Glen Ellyn, IL 60137

- Whole-Brain Thinking Network
  2075 Buffalo Creek Road
  Lake Lure, NC 28746
  704-625-9153; FAX 704-625-2190

D. SELECTED READINGS

- Amabile, Teresa N. *Growing Up Creative—Nurturing a Lifetime of Creativity.* New York: Crown Publishers, 1989.

- Bennett, John G. *Creative Thinking.* Oxford: University Press, 1964.

- Biohowiak, Donald W. *Mavericks: How to Lead Your Staff to Think Like Einstein, Create Like Da Vinci, and Invent Like Edison.* Irwin IL: Business One, 1992.

- Buzon, Tony. *Use Both Sides of Your Brain.* New York: Dutton, 1983.

- Campbell, David. *Take the Road to Creativity and Get Off Your Dead End.* Greensboro, NC: Center for Creative Leadership, 1985.

- Cooper, R. G. *Winning at New Products: Strategy & Process.* Redding, MA: Addison-Wessley, 1993.

- Dailey, Nils L. *Profiles in Management: Roles of the Value-Adding Manager.* N. L. Dailey Associates, 1987.

- de Bono, Edward. *de Bono's Course in Thinking.* New York: Facts on File Publications, 1981.

- de Bono, Edward. *de Bono's Thinking Course.* New York: Facts on File Publications, 1985.

- de Bono, Edward. *I Am Right, You Are Wrong.* New York: Viking Penguin, 1991.

- de Bono, Edward. *The Mechanism of Mind.* New York: Viking Penguin, 1969.

- de Bono, Edward. *Six Thinking Hats.* Boston: Little, Brown & Co., 1985.

- de Bono, Edward. *Serious Creativity.* New York: Harper Collins, 1992.

- de Bono, Edward. *Surpetition—Going Beyond Competition.* New York: Harper Collins, 1992.

- Drucker, Peter P. *Innovation and Entrepreneurship.* New York: Harper & Row, 1985.

- Forster, Richard. *Innovation: The Attacker's Advantage.* New York: Summit Books, 1986.

- Glassman, Edward. *Creativity Handbook: Shift Paradigms and Harvest Creative Thinking at Work.* Chapel Hill, NC: The LSC Press, 1991.

- Herrmann, Ned. *The Creative Brain.* Lake Lure, NC: Brain Books, 1988.

- Herrmann, Ned. *The Whole-Brain Business Book.* New York: McGraw Hill, 1996.

- Kanter, Rosabeth Moss. *The Change Masters: Innovation for Productivity in the American Corporation.* New York: Simon & Schuster, 1983.

- Katzenbach, J. P. and D. K. Smith. *The Wisdom of Teams.* Cambridge, MA: Harvard Business School Press, 1993.

- Kirton, Michael. *Adaptions and Innovations—Styles of Creativity and Problem Solving.* New York: Routledge, 1989.

- McGrath, M. E., M. T. Anthony, and A. R. Shapiro. *Product Development Success Through Product and Cycle-Time Excellence.* Newton, MA: Butterworth-Heinemenn, 1992.

- Miller, William C. *The Creative Edge: How to Foster Innovation Where You Work.* Redding, MA: Addison-Wesley, 1986.

- Osborn, Alex F. *Applied Imagination: Principles and Procedures of Creative Problem-Solving.* New York: Charles Scribner's Sons, 1953.

- Parnes, Sidney J. *Source Book for Creative Problem Solving.* Buffalo, NY: Creative Education Foundation Press, 1992.

- Pinchot, Gifford III. *The End of Bureaucracy and the Rise of the Intelligent Organization.* San Francisco, CA: Berrett-Koehler, 1993.

- Pinchot, Gifford III. *Intrapreneuring: Why You Don't Have to Leave the Corporation to Become an Entrepreneur.* New York: Harper & Row, 1986.

- Prince, George. *The Practice of Creativity: A Manual for Group Problem Solving.* New York: Macmillan, 1970.

- Prather, Charles W. and Lisa K. Gundry. *Blueprints for Innovation.* NY: AMA Membership Publications Division, 1995.

- Shallcross, Doris J. and Dorothy A. Sisk. *Intuition: An Inner Way of Knowing.* Buffalo, NY: Bearly Limited, 1989.

- Smith, P. G. and D. J. Reinertsen. *Developing Products in Half the Time.* New York: Van Nostrand Reinhold, 1991.

- Stein, Morris I. *Making the Point—Anecdotes, Poems & Illustrations for the Creative Process.* Amagansett, NY: The Mews Press, 1984.

- Stein, Morris I. *Stimulating Creativity; Volume I—Individual Procedures.* Amagansett, NY: The Mews Press, 1974.

- Stein, Morris I. *Stimulating Creativity; Volume II—Group Procedures.* Amagansett, NY: The Mews Press, 1975.

- von Oech, Roger. *A Kick in the Seat of the Pants.* New York: Harper & Row, 1986.

- von Oech, Roger. *A Whack on the Side of the Head: How to Unlock Your Mind for Innovation.* New York: Warner Books, 1982.

- Wheelwright, S. C., and Clark, K. B. *Revolutionizing Product Development.* New York: The Free Press, 1992.

- Wycoff, Joyce. *Mind Mapping: Your Personal Guide to Exploring Creativity and Problem Solving.* New York: Berkley Publishing Group, 1991.

REFERENCES

1. Will Durant, *The Story of Philosophy: The Lives & Opinions of the Great Philosophers* (New York: Simon & Schuster, 1967).

2. Edward Glassman, *Creativity Handbook: Shift Paradigms and Harvest Creative Thinking at Work* (Chapel Hill, NC: The LCS Press, 1991).

3. Rolf C. Smith Jr., and Raymond A. Slesinski, "Continuous Innovation," *Executive Excellence Magazine,* May 1991.

4. Edward de Bono, *Mechanism of Mind* (Des Moines, IA: Advanced Practical Thinking Training, Inc.®, 1992).

5. Edward de Bono, *The Use of Lateral Thinking* (Toronto: Penguin Books, 1990).

6. Edward de Bono, *Lateral Thinking Step by Step* (New York: Harper & Row,1970).

7. Edward de Bono, *Lateral Thinking for Management* (London: Penguin Books Ltd., 1971).

8. Edward de Bono, *de Bono's Thinking Course* (New York: Facts on File, 1981).

9. Edward de Bono, *Serious Creativity* (London: Harper Collins, 1992).

10. Advanced Practical Thinking Training, Inc.®, 10520 New York Avenue, Des Moines, IA 50322, Phone: 800-621-3366, Fax: 515-278-2245.

11. The McQuaig Group Inc.®, 132 Rochester Ave., Toronto, Ontario, Canada M4N 191, Fax: 416-488-4544.

12. W. J. J. Gordon, *Synectics* (New York: Harper & Row, 1961).

13. George M. Prince, *The Practice of Creativity* (New York: Macmillan Publishing Co., 1970).

14. Synectics, Inc., 20 University Road, Cambridge, MA 02138.

15. W. J. J. Gordon, *The Metaphorical Way of Learning and Knowing* (Cambridge, MA: Porpoise Books, 1971).

16. W. J. J. Gordon and Tony Poze, *The Metaphorical Way of Learning and Knowing* (Cambridge, MA SES Assoc., May 1979).

17. Donald W. MacKinnon, *Sigmund Freud, Carl Jung, and Otto Rank: Some Implications of Their Work for the Understanding of Creativity* (Berkeley, CA: University of California).

18. DuPont OZ Creative Thinking Network, *Are We Creative Yet?* (Wilmington, DE: DuPont, 1990).

19. Alex F. Osborn, *Applied Imagination: Principles and Procedures of Creative Problem-Solving* (New York: Charles Scribner's Sons, 1979).

20. Tony Buzon, *Use Both Sides of Your Brain* (New York: Dutton,1983).

21. Joyce Wycoff, *Mind Mapping: Your Personal Guide to Exploring Creativity and Problem Solving* (New York: Berkley Publishing Group, 1991).

22. R. F. Eberle, *SCAMPER* (East Aurora, NY: Games for Imagination Development).

23. Edward de Bono, *Six Thinking Hats* (Boston: Little, Brown & Co., 1985).

24. Scott G. Isaksen, Brian Dorval, and Donald Treffinger, *Creative Approaches to Problem Solving* (Dubuque, IA: Kendall Hunt, 1994).

25. Sydney Parnes, *Sourcebook for Creative Problem Solving* (Buffalo, NY: Creative Education Foundation Press, 1992).

26. Edward de Bono, *CoRT Thinking* (Des Moines, IA: Advanced Practical Thinking Training, Inc.®, 1995).

27. Marilyn Schoeman Dow, Thinklink, 2515 39th Ave. SW, Seattle, WA 98116.

28. Ned Herrmann, *The Creative Brain* (Lake Lure, NC: Brain Books, 1988).

29. The Ned Herrmann Group, 2075 Buffalo Creek Rd., Lake Lure, NC 28746.

30. Michael J. Kirton, *Adaptors and Innovators: Styles of Creativity and Problem Solving* (London: Routledge, 1994).

31. Michael J. Kirton, Occupational Research Center, Highlands, Gravel Path, Berkhamsted, Hertfordshire, UK HP4 2PQ.

32. Charles W. Prather, "Risks and Rewards," *Executive Excellence*, January 1992.

33. Gifford Pinchot III, Internal DuPont report, 1986.

34. Scott G. Isaksen, K. J. Lauer, M. C. Murdock, K. B. Dorval, and G. J. Puccio, "The Situational Outlook Questionnaire: Understanding the Climate for Creativity and Change", Technical Manual (Buffalo, NY: CPS Group, 1995).

35. Caleb S. Atwood and Rolf C. Smith Jr., "Creative Practices Survey;" *Consensus*, Vol. 4, No. 2, December 1990.

36. Teresa M. Amabile and Stanley S. Gryskiewicz, "Creativity in the R & D Laboratory," Technical Report #30 (Greensboro, NC: Center for Creative Leadership, 1987).

37. M. E. McGrath, M. T. Anthony, and A. R. Shapiro, *Product Development: Success Through Product and Cycle-Time Excellence* (Newton, MA: Butterworth-Heinemann, 1992).

38. Eugene E. Magat, *In the Pursuit of Strength—The Birth of Kevlar®*, Internal DuPont publication, planned for issuance by Management of Advanced Fibers Systems, 1996.

39. David Tanner, Jim A. Fitzgerald, and Brian R. Phillips, *Kevlar®—From Laboratory to Marketplace Through Innovation*, the DuPont Company Advanced Materials Conference, Wilmington, DE, November 1988.

40. David Tanner, Jim A. Fitzgerald, and Brian R. Phillips, "The Kevlar® Story—An Advanced Materials Case History," *Angev. Chem., Adv. Mater.*, 101, Nr. 5, 1989.

INDEX